The Senate Speeches of

W. B. YEATS

edited by
DONALD R. PEARCE

FABER AND FABER
24 Russell Square
London

*First published in England in mcmlxi
by Faber and Faber Limited
24 Russell Square London WC1
Printed in Great Britain by
Latimer Trend & Co Ltd Whitstable
All rights reserved*

Acknowledgment is here made to the following publishers
for permission to use copyright material in this book:
Macmillan & Co. Ltd., for extracts from the poems "Death,"
"Blood and the Moon" and "A Dialogue of Self and Soul"
from *The Collected Poems of W. B. Yeats*; *The Spectator*, for
Yeats's essay "The Irish Censorship;" The Controller of the
Stationery Office, Government of Ireland, for the essay
"What We Did or Tried to Do."

PREFACE

No PART of Yeats's career has received less scrutiny from his biographers than his six years in the Irish Senate. With the exception of a brief extract from his speech on Divorce, all of Yeats's remarks as a senator have remained unread, buried in the columns of *Seanad Eireann,* the official report of the Senate. This is doubly unfortunate; for an accurate knowledge of his political career is important not only for his biography, but also for the light which it sheds on the growth and development of his powers as a poet. It was, one recalls, during the period of his Senate service that Yeats finally arrived at that syntax of "public speech" which gives to his later work so much of its characteristic eloquence and power.

A further consideration presided over the preparation of this volume. Irish senators were at liberty to make minor revisions of their remarks before copy was returned to the government printing office; this was a privilege not infrequently exercised by Yeats, in consequence of which his Senate speeches are properly part of the canon of his published work. I have aimed, therefore, to establish a reliable text, and have checked each passage not only against the official text in the volumes of *Seanad Eireann* (I-X), but also, through the generosity of

5

Mrs. Yeats, against Yeats's personal copies of the Senate Report, in which he made occasional marginal and interlinear revisions.

With the exception of half a dozen sentences having a purely clerical significance—an isolated query as to a date, a motion for a vote of thanks—all of Yeats's speeches in the Senate are included in the present edition. Nothing has been omitted that might be of conceivable importance to the student of his work. In the case of two or three of the debates, I have found it both expedient and instructive to quote the words of other senators, sometimes fairly extensively; and one debate—enshrining what is probably Yeats's forensic showpiece —I decided to give practically in its entirety, partly as the best way of incorporating necessary information, and partly to preserve the context of excitement attending the occasion. The words of all those senators have, of course, long since become a part of history; but I would record my gratitude for the opportunity to quote them here.

I wish especially to express sincere thanks to Mrs. W. B. Yeats for permission to collect her husband's speeches, and for many a particular kindness and courtesy extended to me while I was in Dublin. I am much indebted to the Horace H. Rackham School of Graduate Studies, University of Michigan, for the award of its Alfred H. Lloyd Post-Doctoral Fellowship which enabled me to live in Dublin; and to the Committee on Research, University of California, Santa Barbara, for financial assistance with the typing. The materials in the several appendices, illustrating different aspects of Yeats's work in the Senate, are reprinted here from their original places of publication for the first time; to the editors of those publications I make the customary grateful acknowledgments.

DONALD R. PEARCE

University of California
Santa Barbara

CONTENTS

Appendices

Illustrations between pages 30 and 31:

W. B. Yeats during His Senate Years
The Irish Coinage

INTRODUCTION

W. B. YEATS became a member of the Irish Senate on December 11, 1922, one of three Senators appointed to advise the government on matters concerning education, literature, and the arts. His first action on being sworn in was almost legendarily Yeatsian: he inspected his own and the country's future by consulting the stars. The horoscope which he cast, based on the exact moment at which he had taken the oath of office, indicated, with notable plausibility, rising trouble for the Free State over the next six years, but announced personal safety for himself. Having ascertained in this fashion the grand outlines of his new career, as well as that of the Senate, he proceeded to devote himself with evident satisfaction to the work of government—"the slow exciting work," he once called it, "of creating institutions."

The phrase was accurate. The first few years of the Free State were years of fundamental political and moral reconstruction. The nation had just passed through a tragic period of guerrilla warfare with England, only to be plunged into a two-year civil war involving shooting of civilians, reprisals, burning of famous houses, bitterness and slander in the opposed presses, and damage to property in the amount of 30 million pounds sterling. Under De Valera's leadership the "Irregulars" (the extreme wing of the Republican Party that had refused to accept the treaty with England) had begun to terrorize the south of Ireland claiming that "this is a continuation of the former war [against England]; the only difference is that in the earlier period England was maintaining her claims directly, now she is maintaining them indirectly through Irishmen." When the war finally came to an end, guerrilla activity and the threat of counterrevolution continued: fourteen categories of people who were considered guilty of real or imagined offenses against Irish freedom—as the Irregulars conceived it—including many of the members of the new government, were on the Irregulars' lists of persons to be shot at sight.

Such was the setting in which the Free State government held its early meetings. But it was particularly unhealthy to be a senator. Not only were senators apt to be vulnerable property owners, but it was well known that many of them at the time of the Provisional Government had favored the setting up of military courts with the power of inflicting the death penalty on Irregulars. Partly for these reasons, and partly as a matter of general precaution, Yeats and a few other senators were instrumental in having the Senate moved from its temporary quarters in the National Museum, because their very presence in the building literally put the national treasures in jeopardy.

Though he was never a violent man, Yeats was exhilarated by the violent events and personalities surrounding him during that period; and years later he was to recall with pride and nostalgia in an article for the *Spectator* how members of that first Senate "went in danger of their lives; some had their houses burnt; country gentlemen came from the blackened ruins of their houses to continue without melodrama or complaint some perhaps highly technical debate in the Senate. . . ." Five years earlier, in 1927, he had concentrated those feelings in a single heroic image in a poem written shortly after the assassination of his friend Kevin O'Higgins, Minister of Justice and External Affairs:

A great man in his pride
Confronting murderous men
Casts derision upon
Supersession of breath;
He knows death to the bone—
Man has created death.

II

The Constitution adopted in 1922 by the first Parliament of the Irish Free State provided for the creation of two houses, the Dáil, or lower house, and the Seanad, or Senate. As originally designed, the Senate numbered sixty members, thirty of whom were elected for a period of three years by the Dáil, and thirty appointed for six years by the President of the Executive Council in consultation with certain legal and commercial groups. (The chief object here was the obtaining of a conservative personnel.) In President Cosgrave's phrase, the Senate was expected to "review and act as a sort of jury on the work of the Dáil;" it could initiate legislation on all matters excepting finance, but could reject no proposal that had been passed by the Dáil.

These arrangements did not work out as smoothly as the President had hoped. The second chamber proved to be not only keenly interested in government, but inconveniently critical as well—it was only a matter of days before it was refusing to pass bills from the Dáil. One such deadlock occurred in connection with the British Indemnity Bill (1923), which proposed to indemnify British police for acts committed during the notorious Black and Tan period. The Senate refused to pass the bill until the British Government made the reciprocal concession of releasing Irish soldiers still lying in English jails. The President urged the Senate to reconsider, pointing out that the Dáil, being more representative of public opinion than the Senate, was the proper chamber from which such an objection should come—a remark almost intuitively calculated to stiffen the Senate's attitude. Part of Yeats's comments on this occasion (January 21, 1923) put the view of the Senate concisely:

. . . I think it is also very important to this Seanad because of the very nature of its constitution, that we should show ourselves as interested as the Dáil is in every person in this country. We do not represent constituencies; we are drawn together to represent certain forms of special knowledge, certain special interests, but we are just as much passionately concerned in these great questions as the Dáil.

Constitutional specifications for senators had required that they be "citizens who shall be proposed on the grounds that they have done honour to the Nation by useful public service or that, because of special qualifications or attainments they represent important aspects of the Nation's life." (Article 30.) Intellectual and artistic matters appeared to be covered by this article, and it was agreed to include a "Cultural Panel" in the Senate. For such a post Yeats, as the most distinguished living Irish man of letters, had been an obvious choice; and when the appointment was offered to him he accepted with pleasure and enthusiasm. His biographers have attributed his senatorship less to his literary distinction than to the fact that he had once belonged to the Irish Republican Brotherhood;* but two members of the then Supreme Council of the I.R.B. with whom I have talked feel that Yeats's connection with that organization would have had little, if any, practical bearing on his appointment to the Senate—particularly since he had never taken the I.R.B. oath, and had "resigned" as early as 1901. One of the two men who proposed Yeats's name to President Cosgrave concurs in this view.

The efficient cause of Yeats's Senate appointment seems rather to have been the partisan energy of his friend Oliver Gogarty. Gogarty

---

* See, for instance, Joseph Hone, *W. B. Yeats: 1865-1939* (New York, 1943), 374; and A. Norman Jeffares, *W. B. Yeats, Man and Poet* (London, 1949), 231.

had been very active during the civil war and was on close personal terms with many of the Free State leaders. When the Senate was being formed he succeeded in convincing Cosgrave of the desirability of giving recognition to the Irish literary movement on the ground that it was, in the succinct wording of the constitution, "an important part of the Nation's life." Stubborn Dublin tradition goes on to insist that Gogarty also defended Yeats's name before the nominating committee when a troubled member queried why a poet should be given a political office in the Irish Free State? Gogarty's retort was swift, and in the grand manner: "If it had not been for W. B. Yeats there would be no Irish Free State!"

It is not surprising that the subtler connections between poetry and nationality which Yeats had sought to promote in Ireland by recreating the cultural traditions of the nation, and filling the public imagination with historic and legendary persons and places, should remain obscure to the mind of a government official. But the more overt connections would have been hard to miss. His early plays, for instance, had had the effect of converting to the National movement certain young men, among them some poets and writers associated with the literary movement, who later died securing the political independence of their country from England in 1916. One of the members of the seven-man Supreme Council of the I.R.B., which had planned that famous Insurrection, tells me that he himself entered the political movement the day after he saw the opening performance of Yeats's *Cathleen ni Houlihan* in April, 1902, prior to which he "had never had a political thought."

Yeats's nationalism was a lifelong passion; and no revolutionary desired Irish freedom more fervently than he, or worked more persistently to help bring it about. But he knew what political revolutionaries are less apt than poets to know or understand—that unity without culture is valueless, or even vicious. The problem, therefore, was to effect value-changes in the Irish *imagination,* and to do it before, rather than after, revolutionary changes in her political structure; otherwise Irish freedom might not be worth the having. For, as his mentor John O'Leary, the Fenian, had insisted many years before, "life is greater than the cause."

Early in his career he had thought it possible to unify Ireland by cultural means. In order to "win the people again," he said in 1901, Irish artists must "take upon [themselves] the methods and the fervour of a priesthood."

I would have our writers and craftsmen of many kinds master this history and these legends, and fix upon their memory the appearance of mountains and rivers and make it all visible again in their arts, so that Irishmen, even though they had gone thousands of miles away, would still be in their own country.

But though the political movement finally culminated in Irish independence, the unified culture which was to have been the crowning fulfillment, not just of the current nationalism but of seven heroic centuries of struggle as well, failed to materialize; the work had ended, like his own Tower, in ruins at the top.

To Yeats, one of the main causes of that failure was the triumph of political democracy. Democracy seemed to him a crude middle-class mechanism by which power and leadership were systematically passed from the mediocre to the incompetent, until the national heritage lay wasted:

And haughtier-headed Burke that proved the State a tree,
That this unconquerable labyrinth of the birds, century after century,
Cast but dead leaves to mathematical equality.

Attached to the tree, the leaves were formal individuals in a living three-dimensional world; on the ground, they were two-dimensional objects in the prostrate world of Euclidian space. He came to hate democracy with an aristocratic hate, and to yearn for strong, but enlightened, political controls. But his authoritarianism, though emphatic and at times exasperated, was never cynical or merely truculent; it was not the authoritarianism of a system, but the authority of the individual, in the face of, or in defiance of, all system. In his later days, the idea of hand-picking officials of state, rather than accepting what "the tide" tossed up as representatives, more and more appealed to him. This sentiment was strengthened by his experiences in the Senate, and his last speech (July 18, 1928), reflects that growing conviction: "I think we should not lose sight of the simple fact that it is more desirable and more important to have able men in this House than to get representative men into this House."

As his biographers have pointed out, Yeats associated with the more conservative elements in the Senate, particularly the Southern Unionists —a group of nationalists who had been in favor of retaining legislative union with Great Britain—led by his father's friend Andrew Jameson, the Dublin distiller. This association appears to have been as personal as it was political in motive, and there seems to be no good reason for doubting Yeats's remark, made later in *On the Boiler,* "I knew that he [Jameson] would leave me free to speak my mind." His speeches bear him out. He frequently voted against the group, and sometimes spoke in opposition to motions introduced by its members. Certainly his speech on Divorce would not have been endorsed by Jameson's followers: its outspoken anticlericalism and defiant Anglo-Irishism combined to render him an eloquent minority of one on that remarkable occasion. His first biographer, Joseph Hone, proposes another reason for his attachment to the Jameson group, and it has the ring of truth: "He wished to insinuate into the ex-Ascendancy Senators a nationalism conceived imaginatively as their heritage from the magnanimity of Swift, Burke and Grattan, 'who gave though free to refuse.'" Hone goes on to remark that "The Senators of the group often sought his advice on practical matters, and one of them said: 'Yeats would have made an admirable banker,' and another, 'A great lawyer was lost in the poet.'"[*]

[*] J. M. Hone, "Yeats as Political Philospher," *The London Mercury,* March, 1939, 494.

His work in the Senate, however, was not much concerned with financial or legal matters, or even with political matters in the usual sense, but with Irish cultural interests; and in this sphere he headed three main Senate Committees. The Irish Manuscript Committee (1923-24) was formed to promote research in Gaelic language, music, folklore, and ancient poetry, and to compile and publish an adequate dictionary of the older language. The Coinage Committee, 1926-28, obtained the beautiful designs of the present Irish currency.* The Committee for the "Federation of the Arts" in Ireland sought to establish a College of the Arts along the lines of the Swedish Royal Academy, with which Yeats had been impressed when he went to Stockholm to receive the Nobel Prize for Literature in 1924. No doubt the Academy stirred memories of his youthful plans for founding an artistic priesthood at Castle Rock in the middle of Lough Key; but, even though he had come to power of a sort, the enterprise met with ministerial indifference, and he abandoned it in 1926.

Yeats engaged in numerous other activities in the Senate for the promotion and protection of the arts in Ireland. He led the renewed but unsuccessful attempt to recover the great Hugh Lane collection of French paintings held on a legality by the National Gallery in London. His persistence and eloquence were decisive in getting the government to draft a new literary Copyright Law. He was effective in securing the preservation of many a national monument endangered by construction programs or by neglect. He gave considerable time and thought to education in the Irish secondary schools and proposed some basic reforms. In 1926, under the auspices of the Senate, he visited some schools in the south of Ireland; and it was one of these visits, to a Catholic school in Waterford, that provided the occasion of his great meditative poem *Among School Children*.

He found Irish schools on the whole "not fit places for children, insanitary, out of repair" and he called for the immediate construction of modern school buildings and the devising of a new and integrated

* See Yeats's witty account of the committee's work in the Appendix.

curriculum that would seem "one lesson and not a mass of unrelated topics." Speaking before the Irish Literary Society in December, 1925,* he urged Irish teachers to

feed the immature imagination upon [the] old folk life, and the mature intellect upon Berkeley and the great modern idealist philosophy created by his influence, upon Burke who restored to political thought its sense of history, and Ireland is reborn, potent, armed and wise. Berkeley proved that the world was a vision, and Burke that the State was a tree, no mechanism to be pulled in pieces and put up again, but an oak tree that had grown through the centuries.

He urged educators to make religion central to the curriculum and to teach it as "a part of history and of life itself, a part, as it were, of the foliage of Burke's tree"—not as "an abstract thing, like those Graeco-Roman casts upon the shelves in the art-schools, but as part of [the child's] emotional life." These thoughts presently became song, fashioning for themselves a magnificent image in the religious and political "great-rooted blossomer" of *Among School Children,* its roots deep in history and folklore, and its Burkean trunk lifting civic branches crowned with Berkeley's Idealism.

But the majority of the debates were not on such stimulating topics. Very often they were on matters which it is practically impossible to imagine Yeats being much interested in—Oil in Navigable Waters, Subsidy for Fat Cattle, Civil Service Regulations. Some of the meetings were dull and tedious in the extreme. Nevertheless, he attended over sixty per cent of the Senate meetings—the average for senators was fifty per cent—which was a creditable attendance, particularly in view of the fact that his health required him to spend most of each winter away from Ireland. The image of these meetings that remained in his mind in after years was understandably bleak: "Some old banker, or lawyer," he wrote, "would dominate the House, leaning upon the back of the chair in front, always speaking with undisturbed self-

* See Appendix IV for the complete draft of this lecture.

possession as at some table in a board room." But sometimes, perhaps once or twice a year, the debates were on matters directly affecting the liberty of the mind in Ireland, or the arts, and at such times he was vocal enough—"incisive" and "convincing" are the words used to describe his speeches by fellow senators still living. Occasionally, as in the case of his carefully prepared speech on Divorce, he edged his remarks with a reckless eloquence of phrase that is still remembered in Dublin; on that memorable occasion he scandalized the House, though in its heart of hearts it must have been more than a little entertained, for it was a remarkably urbane body in those days, and its members shared a taste for the theatrical. The peroration of his Divorce speech was not unworthy of Grattan:

... I think it is tragic that within three years of this country gaining its independence we should be discussing a measure which a minority of this nation considers to be grossly oppressive. I am proud to consider myself a typical man of that minority. We against whom you have done this thing are no petty people. We are one of the great stocks of Europe. We are the people of Burke; we are the people of Grattan; we are the people of Swift, the people of Emmet, the people of Parnell. We have created the most of the modern literature of this country. We have created the best of its political intelligence. Yet I do not altogether regret what has happened. I shall be able to find out, if not I, my children will be able to find out whether we have lost our stamina or not. You have defined our position and given us a popular following. If we have not lost our stamina then your victory will be brief, and your defeat final, and when it comes this nation may be transformed.

Ordinarily, Yeats did not put this much craftsmanship into the composition of his speeches. According to Mrs. Yeats, with whom I had the pleasure of discussing his working habits, he usually enjoyed an afternoon spent putting a speech together. Once she evoked for me a charming picture. Yeats would stride, tall and silver-haired, up and down the length of his study, shaping and rehearsing a passage, dictating it to her when it satisfied his ear, now and then breaking into laughter over some witty phrase, or mischievous illustration of a point:

Now, I have spoken very seriously, but I want to turn from seriousness to a fact which has been burning in my imagination since this meeting began—a discovery I made which has lightened this serious subject for me. I have been looking for a historical precedent for the remarkable fact that certain Englishmen who afterwards became Cabinet Ministers and in other ways rose to the highest positions in the State went over to Ulster about 15 years ago and armed the people at a time of entire peace and urged them, and are now urging them, to use these arms against us. I have found a historical precedent which establishes that it is an old custom of the British Government. I have found that Edmund Burke in the middle of the eighteenth century drew attention to a very remarkable item in the Estimates of the year. It was an item of so much money for the purchase of five gross of scalping knives, which scalping knives were intended to be given to the American Indians that they might scalp the French.

During the debate on the valuable Lane collection of modern French paintings, held on a formality by the National Gallery in London, Yeats made a bold and ingenious proposal for their recovery by Ireland:

. . . In the midst of the Great War, by Act of Parliament, the will of Cecil Rhodes was modified. In that case there was no question of the letter of the will or of his intentions. He had left a large bequest to enable German students to attend certain English universities. They abrogated that request not merely for the time of the war but for ever. That is precisely one of those actions which all nations do in time of war and are ashamed of afterwards. Yet it seems to me if we had claimed that we would not make an excessive claim. It seems to me what they did by Act of Parliament to modify the will of Cecil Rhodes under the influence of national hatred they might well be asked to do—to modify the will of Sir Hugh Lane under the influence of national honour. Now what are we to do? No compromise. We ask and we must continue to ask our right—to hold 39 pictures, and for ever. Let the Dublin Commissioners build that long-promised gallery. We have already, in Harcourt Street, great treasures that will make it one of the richest galleries in the world. Let them build that gallery and let them see there is ample space for these 39 pictures. Let them write the names of the pictures on the wall, in spaces reserved for them, and let the codicil be displayed in some conspicuous place and watch the public opinion of these countries. I do not believe that the public opinion of these countries will permit the London Gallery to retain pictures which it was not the intention of the donor to leave to it.

There is clearly little danger, in reading these speeches, of forming an excessively political image of Yeats and losing sight of the man and poet. He always spoke in his true character. His humanity suffered no contraction in the Senate: government work only provided new occasions for his personality to express itself, from debates on bills of national importance to minute personal encounters. A former senator, who is now an official of the National Library in Dublin, once recalled for me a touching incident. A few years before he entered the Senate, this young man had published a small, unnoticed volume of poems. By the time he became a senator, however, he had abandoned the idea of devoting himself to poetry—but Yeats's presence in the Senate literally filled him with awe. One afternoon, during a recess in one of the meetings, Yeats came over to where the young senator was seated, sat down beside him and to his astonishment opened the conversation with "We poets are not much at home in this kind of work."

Many of the speeches in this volume were, of course, simply duty speeches, never composed with the idea of their being carefully preserved and savoured years afterwards by scholars in universities. Yet it is one measure of his achievement, of his personal as well as of his artistic greatness—for he was a very great man as well as a very great poet—that fairly routine utterances of his should possess the power to fascinate and to move us simply because he spoke them. Mrs. Yeats once explained to me that he was accustomed to distinguish those pages of manuscript that were to be discarded from those that were to be kept and filed by referring to the latter as *"history"*; early drafts of certain poems, abandoned ideas for a play, alternative versions of some essay—all had their place in an intellectual and personal "history" that was as objective to his scrutiny as if it were not his own but the life of another man. It is as part of that "history" that even his minor speeches properly lay claim to our attention. His more serious speeches are important to the understanding of his convictions about both literature and politics, and invite a re-evaluation of both sides of his career. Students of Yeats's poetry will, for instance, be particularly interested in the following speeches: 11. Irish Manuscripts, 1923; 12. The Lane Pictures, 1923; 32. Irish Manuscripts, 1924; 49., 51., 53., 54. Copyright Protection, 1927.

One should remember when reading the non-literary speeches that it was after all a poet, not a professional statesman, who made them; a poet, moreover, of whom it was uniquely true that no personal experience—least of all six years as an Irish politician—was ever likely to be lost on him, or turned to no account in his verse. The man who was composing political speeches for the Senate in the afternoons, was spending his mornings building the diction and syntax of *The Tower* and *The Winding Stair*; and no one was more aware than Yeats himself of the rhetorical and substantial connections between that poetry and those speeches. On the occasion of his Nobel Prize award, he explained to an *Irish Times* reporter:

The aim of all his work had been to perfect what he describes as the syntax of passionate speech. One ought to be able to declaim a lyric, he said, in a market square, so that the people who heard it hardly would realize that they were not listening to prose. Wordsworth had broken new ground by his discovery of the vocabulary of such speech. Ernest Dowson, Lionel Johnson and himself—he, perhaps more consciously than the other two, for he was more of a philosopher—had striven to find its syntax.

One need only select at random to illustrate:

> A living man is blind and drinks his drop.
> What matter if the ditches are impure?
> What matter if I live it all once more?
> Endure that toil of growing up;
> The ignominy of boyhood; the distress
> Of boyhood changing into man;
> The unfinished man and his pain
> Brought face to face with his own clumsiness . . .

The dramatic, attention-seizing rhythms, the direct and forceful syntax, transfer the reader to an auditorium; one is addressed in song.

The image of Yeats in the Irish Senate has another meaning that is not without significance for cultural history. In the debate on divorce legislation the following extraordinary exchange occurs:

COL. MOORE: . . . He [Yeats] quotes the poet Milton as an authority. I do not know whether the poet Milton ever wrote on divorce.

DR. YEATS: One of the most famous of all the prose works of Milton is on divorce which the Senator should have been taught at school.

On the face of it, this is comedy. It is amusing to think of one senator on the floor of the House reproving another senator for being unfamiliar with an essay by John Milton. Government officials surely have more to do with their time than to pore over the works of Renaissance poets. Then it suddenly ceases to amuse. One begins to wonder whom, in fact, the senator ought to have read on divorce if not John Milton? And what else of comparable weight and magnitude has the senator, who is about to frame our laws, not been taught at school? How does it come about that people who have not read the basic philosophical and imaginative texts of our civilization get into office anyway? It is a rare thing today for a government official to introduce Milton or some other soaring literary or philosophical work into a parliamentary debate; it might very well undo his credit with the House as a serious man of affairs.

But Yeats cited Milton on the floor of the Irish Senate with pride, not once but several times; and it is the fact that his having done so is clearly unique that shocks us. Ireland is a small nation and the Irish Senate of 1925 a fairly inconspicuous political body; but size is of no account where questions of universal principle are concerned. It is the singularity of the fact, a poet in the government of a nation, that claims our attention. It is necessary to go back 300 years, to Milton himself, for a like instance of a great imaginative man comparably involved in the political affairs of his country, that is to say, for a like instance of the union of the practical and the meditative intellect. If cultural historians are right, somewhere around the time of Milton there began the ascendancy in our culture of the practical intellect, the religion of certainty, the principle of *quantity,* which though a long time coming into its force is now the dragon law of our life; at the same time there set in a corresponding decline in the prestige of the poetic intelligence and the function of the imaginative man. Yeats's appearance in the Senate of his country compels one, I think, to reflect on the long separation of the man of imagination from the public forum, and of the consequences which that protracted alienation has had, and is having.

III

Yeats retired from the Senate on the 28th of November, 1928, along with several other of the appointed members, without seeking re-election at the "Second Triennial." Some biographers to the contrary, there seems to be no doubt that he could have been elected for a second term if he had wanted it, but his health, which now kept him in the south of France for whole winters, would not let him undertake much public activity; and, anyway, he was temporarily disillusioned with Irish political life. It was no secret that he was disappointed over the declining quality of the men who were now getting into the Senate. Shortly after retiring from political life he admonished Ezra Pound, somewhat ironically one surmises, not to be elected to the Senate of *his* country, because "neither you, nor I, nor any other of our excitable profession can match those old lawyers, old bankers, old business men, who, because all habit and memory, have begun to govern the world." (Pound's response was a bit delayed; but it came eventually, from a detention cage in Pisa twenty years later:

> *If a man don't occasionally sit in a senate*
> *how can he pierce the darrk mind of a*
> > *senator?*)

But Yeats's disillusion with politics was neither consistent nor final. Summing up the achievement of the Free State government in an article for the *Spectator* in 1932, he said: "Nothing remains the same and there have been few mistakes. My six years in the Irish Senate taught me that no London Parliament could have found the time or the knowledge for that transformation. But I am less grateful for what it has done than because its mere existence delivered us from obsession." No Irishman was better qualified than Yeats to speak of Ireland and its government in these terms; for none had struggled longer or in so many ways, of which the senatorship was only one, to free her from obsession.

The Senate Speeches of

W. B. YEATS

You will forgive me if I forget that I am occasionally a politician and remember that I am always a man of letters, and speak less diplomatically and with less respect for institutions and great names than is, perhaps, usual in public life.

W. B. YEATS, *addressing the Irish Senate, July 14, 1926*

FIRST TRIENNIAL PERIOD

December 6, 1922 — December 5, 1925

 DURING the first three years of its existence the Irish Free State saw peace restored to the nation, the financial system put on a solid basis, popular government reestablished, and the emergence of an efficient political organization. The legislative record for the period is impressive: one hundred and thirty bills of the first importance to the country's well-being were drafted, discussed in both Houses, and processed as law. In all these activities the Senate played a strong and effective part, carrying through a total of five hundred amendments to the bills presented to it for passage. Legislation fell into four principal categories in the period: (a) bills relating to national reconstruction, emergency law enforcement, damage to property, personal compensation; (b) bills relating to public health, Civil Service, unemployment; (c) the establishment of various departments of state, ministries and secretaries, the postal service, transportation, courts of justice; (d) cultural matters, such as the Irish language, education, censorship.

Yeats participated in the Senate debates on many of the above topics. But his chief concern was cultural affairs, and except for his address on Divorce, his long speeches were on aspects of the intellectual and artistic life of the nation—the encouragement of Irish scholarship, the study of the older language and literature, the ownership of the great collection of paintings left by Sir Hugh Lane.

1. ELECTION OF SENATE CHAIRMAN

December 12, 1922.

MR. THOMAS MCPARTLIN: . . . I am sorry that the Press has been asked to withdraw. It would be interesting for the people of the country to know that we are all anxious to get the man or woman who has the most ability to conduct our proceedings.

MR. W. B. YEATS: I think we should put aside once and for all all diplomacy in dealing with the people of the country. We have been diplomatized for a generation. Let us stop it. I am in thorough agreement with Colonel Moore when he said we would be judged in this country by our abilities as a Seanad. I suggest we consider nothing whatever but whether the man we are going to choose will have the necessary legal and necessary political knowledge to steer this Seanad through the exceedingly intricate channels through which it will have to pass. We have thorny legal questions in this Seanad on every side of us, and, of course, we will have thorny political questions. The past is dead not only for us but for this country. There is no individual whom we can appoint who will add in any way to our popularity.* What enemy of ours will lay down his gun because of any man we

---

* Yeats was speaking in support of Lord Glenavy's nomination for Chairman of the Senate. Lord Glenavy had been a lifelong Unionist and had opposed Home Rule. He was, however, a very distinguished lawyer and proved an ideal chairman of the Senate from 1922 to 1928.

W. B. YEATS DURING HIS SENATE YEARS

Courtesy of Mr. Albert LeBrocquy

THE IRISH COINAGE

appoint here? I suggest we are assembled here no longer in a National-ist or Unionist sense, but merely as members of the Seanad. [I, 11-12]

2. STANDING COMMITTEES

January 10, 1923. Colonel Moore's motion was for the formation of a Standing Committee to consider the advisability of establishing Standing Committees to advise the Senate from time to time on such subjects as Finance, Foreign Affairs, Education, and other matters. Colonel Maurice Moore was the brother of George Moore, the Irish novelist, with whom Yeats had been associated in the nineties.

MR. YEATS: I have felt, and I am sure we have all felt, the fact that we are a group of individuals who do not know each other, and that is a great injury to us in our capacity as a deliberative body. I think, at the same time, if Colonel Moore brings this to a vote now it will prob-ably be lost, and I imagine under the new Standing Orders it would not be possible to raise it again for some time. I think it is necessary for us to know something of each other before we form such a Committee on the various subjects suggested by Colonel Moore. I feel it is important that we should not do anything now to injure our chances of carrying out such a project later on. I think, then, we might possibly find it a little desirable to be guided by the idea of not forming Committees on subjects for which there are already Ministries in the Dáil. Now, if we appoint Committees such as those suggested, we may find ourselves in the position of critics of the Dáil, which is not desirable. We might, on the other hand, find it desirable to form Committees for subjects in connection with which there are no Ministries. For instance, Public Health. Now there is no Ministry of Public Health. It might be de-sirable to form Committees of that kind. I am myself anxious to see a Committee appointed to look after the interests of Fine Arts, and I do feel if this motion is brought to a vote it may probably be lost, and if it is not lost we have not sufficient knowledge of each other to form such Committees with the necessary information. I therefore suggest that we postpone this resolution for some time. [I, 115]

> *The motion, amended to include committees of the Dáil as well as of the Senate, was agreed to by the Senate. Yeats was appointed to the Standing Committee.*

3. INDEMNITIES TO BRITISH

January 24, 1923. Indemnity (British Military) Bill. Moved by Colonel Moore that the consideration of this Bill should be adjourned to give the British Government a chance "by a similar gracious act to release every Irish prisoner under its control for a political offence connected with Ireland in whatever country the offence may have been committed." Yeats seconded.

MR. YEATS: I think we must simply act on the information we have, and try and come to a decision that seems right on the arguments before us. If we do cause inconvenience to the Dáil, the Dáil will possibly find some means of putting the facts as they see them before us. We can only act on the facts as they are before us now. I would suggest that we are not making anything in the nature of a threat. We are simply suggesting to England that this amnesty should be made in the most gracious form possible, and that it could only be made in the most gracious form by being made by both countries. I presume that both England and we have the same object, to allay the bitter feeling between these countries, and we have drawn the attention of the English Parliament to an unfortunate oversight on their part. They have omitted to set free certain prisoners whom they have, perhaps, forgotten. We think that this amnesty upon our part will sound better in the ears of our own countrymen if England passes a similar amnesty. I think that is a very fair conclusion to come to. I think it is also very important to this Seanad, because of the very nature of its constitution, that we should show ourselves as interested as the Dáil is in every person in this country. We do not represent constituencies; we are drawn together to represent certain forms of special knowledge, certain special interests, but we are just as much passionately concerned in these great questions as the Dáil. I would suggest, therefore, that we pass this resolution now. [I, 167-68]

Motion carried.

4. LAW ENFORCEMENT

February 8, 1923. Enforcement of law (Occasional Powers) Bill. Moved by Kevin O'Higgins.

MR. W. B. YEATS: I would draw attention to the following:— "Provided, however, that in any case where the Under-Sheriff shall break and enter the premises of a person other than the person against whom he has been called upon to enforce a judgment order or decree he shall either have found any goods, animals or other chattels of such last-mentioned person therein or thereon or shall have reasonable grounds for believing that there were some such goods, animals or chattels therein or thereon."

As I understood from the speech of the minister, this is the clause that has been strengthened. In its original form he was only exempt from action if he did find goods in the house, such as he expected to find. At present he can evade on showing reasonable grounds of suspicion. I raise the point that it is a very serious thing to increase the rights of entry into a house. You have here the case where an officer of the State can enter a house. You increase the rights of entry and that is a serious thing. I do not say that it is wrong to do. At present it seems to me that the bailiff can enter your house and allege that his reason for doing so is that he suspects you of having a clock belonging to a neighbour against whom there is a judgment. I think it is a serious thing to give the bailiff the right to enter your house, possibly by force, because of the suspicion he holds that you have got somebody else's property. Unless there is some very strong reason for it, I would ask the Minister to consider a modification of the clause. [I, 277-78]

> Mr. O'Higgins explained that it was only a slight extension of the existing laws. The government was seeking means of searching houses because civil law was constantly being violated at the hands of the Irregulars by theft, arson, assassinations, intimidations. Shortly after, Yeats spoke a second time.

MR. W. B. YEATS: The general necessity of this Bill leaves in my mind no possibility of doubt. About six months ago I was staying in the country, when a process server arrived to serve a process* on me. I think it was for rates.** He had with him seven Free State soldiers to protect him. I invited him to tea, and he and the Free State soldiers had tea with me, and my wife took their photographs. Shortly afterwards, however, he found himself amongst debtors who were less hospitable, for instead of giving him tea and cake and taking his photograph, they compelled him to eat all his own summonses. There was a large quantity of paper, and paper, I believe, is exceedingly indigestible. On the question of the details of the Bill I have nothing to say, as the representative of the Labour Party has drawn attention to the one clause which rouses my suspicion only because I do not yet know whether there is a very good case for it. [I, 284-85]

* Process: A legal writ or summons.
** Rates: Local property tax.

5. ARTHUR GRIFFITH

March 14, 1923. Griffith Settlement Bill: Interim Stage. Introduced by President Cosgrave to the Dáil, this bill was "intended to make suitable provision for the widow, children and sister of the late President Arthur Griffith, in consideration of his eminent services to the nation. . . ."

MR. W. B. YEATS: I wish to add my voice to that of Senator Colonel Sir Hutcheson Poe. I was on many points deeply opposed to Mr. Arthur Griffith during his lifetime on matters connected with the Arts, but time has justified him on the great issue that most concerns us all. He was a man of the most enduring courage and the most steadfast will. I have good reason for knowing how enduring his courage was. I first met him a great many years ago, when he and his friend Rooney were editing a little paper which they set up with their own hand as well as writing it. They also paid for the weekly expenditure on that paper. I know how hard a struggle it was for him to edit and print that paper, and I remember in those days, on hearing how hard that struggle was, I offered to get some of his articles placed in, I think, "The Speaker" which was an English liberal paper. I remember his reply, that he had taken a vow to himself never to write for any paper outside Ireland. That was for him a vow of poverty, and he kept it. For many years, at least two or three years, before the end, it must have seemed to him that he was carrying on an almost hopeless struggle, and when the final crisis came, he showed himself a man of particular value to this country, if it were only in this, that when the final test came he gave his faith, not to an abstract theory, but to a conception of this historical nation—and we are all theory mad. On that point he kept himself thoroughly sane, and we owe, therefore, to his memory great honour—honour that will always be paid by this country. [I, 470-71]

6. LOCATION OF PARLIAMENT

March 15, 1923. Standing Orders Committee Report. On the permanent location of the Oireachtas (literally, "Assembly"). The legislature of the Irish Free State was composed of a President, Dáil Eireann (Chamber of Deputies), and Seanad Eireann (Senate).

MR. W. B. YEATS: In moving my amendment I am not going to use the form of words which has been circulated. These words are not mine and I do not think them practicable, so I hope I have the leave of the Seanad to use a different form of words which in no way differs in intention from that circulated. I propose that in addition to the message to the Dáil proposed in paragraph five a message be also forwarded requesting that before any final arrangements are made relative to the permanent location of the Oireachtas, including the questions of site, locality, and the allocation of the necessary chambers and offices between the two Houses, a joint conference of members of both Houses be called together to consider this matter. I know, of course, that as this is a matter that involves the expenditure of money, the other House will be entirely within its rights if it refuses to consult us on the matter, but I would think now that it is pointed to them they will decide as a matter of courtesy to consult us, for, after all, it is right that we should know in what manner of house we are going to speak and eat, and, if the state of this country continues to be disturbed, possibly to sleep. I, for one, would very much like to know whether we are to have chairs or benches. I feel strongly in the circumstances in favour of benches. We only know from common rumour, if that can be described as knowledge, where the other House is to be. There is a certain amount of feeling in the country that it should be the House in College Green,* and I am sure that, considering the strength of the

* The beautiful eighteenth-century building across from Trinity College was originally the Irish House of Parliament, now the Bank of Ireland. The government decided at last

case in sentiment and tradition for that House, if the Government has given up that idea they have done so for some sound reason. Then we hear again from public rumour that we are probably going to the Royal Hospital. If that is decided upon I should like to be assured that the Government will take great care of that priceless building, that they will not alter it in any substantial way, and that if they have to add to it, as they will have, they will not so add to it as to destroy its proportions. It is a masterpiece of architecture. It is not only the work of a great architect, but the work of a great architect of a great period. There are also, I know, certain plaster ceilings there, Italian work of great value. But whatever decision they come to they should, as a matter of courtesy, consult us. It would be a matter to us of regret if it is found that the old building in College Green is impossible. I think that there are certain members of the Seanad present whose ancestors took part in the debates in that House, and helped to create one of the few great schools of oratory which has arisen since classical times. I think that if it were upon that ground alone the Government should consult us before it has made any final decision. [I, 531-33]

7. VOTING CARDS

March 22, 1923. Electoral Bill (Committee). On photographs of electors on voting cards.

MR. W. B. YEATS: I merely wish to point out that the proposal contains no suggestion that the photograph need be a recent one. The enterprising elector could put a photograph of himself as a baby on a card and, as all babies look exactly alike to the masculine mind, it will be impossible to say whether it was accurate or not. [I, 619]

to settle in Leinster House, because it would have cost too much to put the older building in College Green into suitable repair.

8. DAMAGE TO PROPERTY

March 28, 1923. Damage to Property Bill: Second Stage.

MR. YEATS: If it comes to a vote on the question of compensation for personal injuries I do not know on which side I am going to vote, because as yet I have heard no defence of the Government position. I have failed to find any defence of the Government's position in the newspapers. I am convinced that they have a defence, because I have found through my life a certain dogma very valuable, "There is no strong case without a strong answer," and the whole country is full of cases for compensation for personal injuries. It is full even of excellent jokes on the subject. I am told that a certain country solicitor, acting for the widow of a murdered man, has sent into the Government a bill for a very badly perforated suit of clothes. Now, I think that the Government which receives with equanimity a claim of that kind has obviously a very strong case indeed, and I hope that the Minister for Finance will give us that case. I am very anxious to be instructed on what side I am to vote. Am I to assist the Seanad to hold up this Bill or not on this most important question? I do not know if I am in agreement with the Senator who is anxious that where a man's house has been burned he should be given the opportunity, instead of rebuilding, of building house property in some neighbouring town. I suggest that that would be an incitement to other men to burn their neighbours' houses and get rid of men who are occupying a certain amount of land that they would like. I also suggest that it is very desirable that any clause in this Bill which encourages a man to rebuild should be kept. This Country will not always be an uncomfortable place for a country gentleman to live in, and it is most important that we should keep in this country a certain leisured class. I am afraid that Labour disagrees with me in that. On this matter I am a crusted

Tory. I am of the opinion of the ancient Jewish book which says "there is no wisdom without leisure." [I, 724]

9. PERSONAL INJURIES

April 18, 1923. Compensation for Personal Injuries. On damages sustained by Irishmen during the Black and Tan and Civil War periods.

MR. W. B. YEATS: In commenting on what the last Senator said [that the intentions of the Government were not clear to the people] I wish to say that a letter appeared in the London Times about three weeks ago from some person acting for refugees, saying the Government was excluding compensation for personal injuries in order that loyalists injured in the late war might be left penniless. I think that is an example of the kind of misunderstanding the Government has to face over this Bill. I do not think any one of us doubts for one moment that the tribunal the Government will set up will be perfectly just in this matter. It is a question of dealing with a country which is exceedingly suspicious, and refugees who are exceedingly suspicious, and the circumstances are such as likely to leave these suspicions in existence for a considerable time. [I, 922-23]

10. LEAGUE OF NATIONS

April 19, 1923. Senator Douglas proposed that Ireland now request admission to the League of Nations. Mr. Jameson objected that the question was too big for immediate decision.

MR. YEATS: I hold the same view as Senator Jameson, and I have risen to ask if it would not be expedient for the Seanad to appoint a committee to go into the whole question especially with a view to considering the question of the Boundary, and as to what extent our entering the League of Nations would commit us to join in a war against our will; there are other most thorny subjects which to me seem to be questions for legal interpretation. I think it highly desirable that we should appoint a Committee with the necessary expert knowledge to report on the subject before we come to a definite decision.

MR. MCPARTLIN: . . . I think the suggestion that Senator Yeats has put forward is the most advisable in order to give us more time and more information before deciding. I appeal to Senator Douglas to consider Senator Yeats' proposal.

SIR NUGENT EVERARD: I move that we pass to the next business.

MR. YEATS: I second the motion.

MR. DOUGLAS: . . . A postponement I could possibly understand, although that is what we did previously; a rejection I could understand; a suggestion that it might be withdrawn I could understand; but a proposal to try to close the discussion on the matter, so as to prevent a reply, I cannot understand, and I cannot understand the object of the proposer and the seconder. . . .

MR. YEATS: I had no intention of being discourteous. I was under the impression that Senator Douglas had replied. I disagree with his criticism that members of this assembly did not properly study the question. They studied it thoroughly.

AN CATHAOIRLEACH:* You are out of order. You have already seconded this motion.

MR. YEATS: I have not spoken on it.

AN CATHAOIRLEACH: That is your misfortune.

MR. YEATS: One can always adjourn one's speech. I think that is so, according to the Standing Orders.

AN CATHAOIRLEACH: With the consent of the Seanad. I will not interfere with you, but strictly you are not in order.

MR. YEATS: I only seconded it formally. I thought it allowed me to

* Gaelic for "Chairman."

4 0

make my speech later, and I still contend that is so under the Standing Orders.

AN CATHAOIRLEACH: As you made no speech beyond formally seconding it, I shall not prevent you speaking now.

MR. YEATS: I have no great knowledge of procedure, and I am sorry if I have blundered into a discourteous procedure. What I had in my mind was that three members of the Seanad had studied the question so thoroughly that they brought it before the Seanad; that we might have the border question settled, and that we might be drawn into war by the League of Nations. It seems to me that these questions require studying, and that they are largely questions of the legal interpretation of clauses, and before we discuss this question we ought to know what experts think of these clauses. I have no opinion on the question one way or another, but I want to know if, as it seems to me, by moving the previous question, and getting rid of a decision, we will not have the opportunity later on of appointing a Committee to consider the legal bearing of the clauses of the League of Nations on this question? (Amendment by leave withdrawn.)

· · · ·

AN CATHAOIRLEACH: We stand now in the position that the original motion by Senator Douglas is still open for discussion or for amendment.

MR. YEATS: I wish to move an amendment "That a committee of this Seanad be appointed to consider whether it is or is not advisable for the Irish Free State to join in the League of Nations."

MR. MCPARTLIN: I have pleasure in seconding. . . .

· · · ·

MR. YEATS: Might I suggest an addition to that that the committee consist of the speakers for and against Senator Douglas's motion, with the addition of the Cathaoirleach of the Seanad?

AN CATHAOIRLEACH: That would be the whole Seanad.

MR. YEATS: The speakers I meant.

AN CATHAOIRLEACH: It would be better to make a selection.

MR. JAMESON: I wonder is it wise to mix up two resolutions like that? The Earl of Wicklow's* is perfectly clear by itself. Now I doubt that it would be a wise thing to appoint a committee to consider a matter of this kind that is not really before us yet. When the Government tells us what they are going to say in reply to the Earl of Wicklow's resolution, and whether we are going to be consulted or not, it will then be time for us to appoint committees and to put our house in order, if it is then considered a wise thing to appoint a Committee at all. I think there are many objections to appointing committees on a great many subjects. Even in Senator Yeats's own proposal he is practically going to appoint members of the Seanad who have already declared their opinion to be against the thing.

MR. YEATS: I withdraw the suggestion. [I, 978-79]

II. IRISH MANUSCRIPTS

April 19, 1923.

MR. YEATS: In the old days in Ireland when we began our imaginative movement which, for good or evil, had a little share in bringing about recent events, we all looked forward to the time when there would be adequate editions of the old literature of Ireland. That literature is of very great importance. The late d'Arbois de Jubainville, a very great Frenchman of science, whom I knew, spent his life in its study on the ground that through that literature you got to know what the world was immediately before Homer. In addition to that there is lyric poetry, great lyric poetry in Irish, lyric literature that was matured in the time of Chaucer. The work I hope the Seanad will

* Senator the Earl of Wicklow's resolution, made earlier in the debate, was that "this Seanad should condemn in no uncertain terms" the Government's apparent decision to seek admission into the League of Nations "without consulting Parliament."

enable the various scholars to do will be a work of science, that is to say a study of a language which is of great importance to culture, and a study of this old literature. It is not a work of propaganda. I am not in any way denying the importance of propaganda, but personally I do not get any pleasure when I see my name spelt in a way that makes it look very strange to me at the top of this resolution. It seems to me that that is a course entirely warranted by recent science. It is the propagandist way of saying: "I am getting better and better." What I propose to you is a work which I think any Government in the world would feel justified in undertaking. Much of this work has already been done by certain bodies, done with very limited resources, by the Royal Irish Academy, Trinity College, the School of Irish Learning and the Irish Texts Society. The greater portion of the Saga literature has already been adequately translated and adequately edited, but there still remains great quantities of old Bardic poetry which should be translated. There is also great need for critical editions of the Annals, the Annals of Boyle, Innisfallen and Connaught, and above all, perhaps, there is need for a dictionary of the old language. I have been in consultation during the last week with the principal Gaelic scholars, or most of them. Mr. Best, Professor MacNeill, Dr. Douglas Hyde, and Mr. Gwynn. I think they are unanimous on the importance of the dictionary. Then, too, as a preliminary work, a proper catalogue is required of the work of the Royal Irish Academy. A very large rough catalogue does exist, but a condensed catalogue is necessary. Trinity College scholars have just published their catalogue, and the British Museum is about to publish its catalogue of Irish Manuscripts there.

The proposal I make will not require a very large sum of money. At the beginning, at any rate, it will be quite a small sum annually, which will be used to keep at their work certain young scholars. I understand that Professor Bergin of the National University has two or three scholars of very great promise. At the moment two of these are studying in Germany with travelling scholarships; I understand Professor O'Rahilly and Professor Gwynn, in Trinity College, have a few more. In ordinary circumstances these scholars would have to accept, let us say, School Inspectorships, or something of that kind, and would be lost to Irish Scholarship. It is most desirable that a little money should be found in order that they should be set to do the work I have described, probably cataloguing in the first place, and dictionary making, and later on, or simultaneously, editing all the old Bardic poetry and bringing out critical editions of the Annals. When I read this resolution, you will find that I have made slight additions to it at the suggestion of certain scholars, chiefly Mr. Best. I may be a little out of order in doing that, but I hope you will permit it. I have added a clause which would permit a certain portion of the money being expended in training scholars in phonetics, so that they would be able to take down what of Irish literature still remains in the living tongue. It is quite possible that that is the most important work of all, because that old literature in songs and stories is dying out. It only exists, I understand, in its perfection where the people still think in Irish. As they become thoroughly bilingual even, it dies away, so that it is work that can be done to-day, and done next year and the year after, but very soon it will be a work which cannot be done at all. That is why, perhaps, it is most pressing.

I feel it strange that I, who am a non-Gaelic scholar, should be left to bring this proposal before the Seanad. I may say, to give a little weight to my words, that the greater portion of my own writings have been founded upon the old literature of Ireland. I have had to read it in translations, but it has been the chief illumination of my imagination all my life. The movement I am connected with, the whole poetic movement of modern Ireland, has drawn a great portion of its inspiration from the old Bardic literature. I think it is of great importance to set before our own people a task which they will feel naturally inclined to undertake. It is a great thing, when you find people wanting to learn anything, that you should encourage them to learn that, and not something else that they do not want to learn.

It is a moment, too, when we will have to build up again the idealism of Ireland. We have had the old form of wild, wasteful historic idealism. The country got into that position, but, like a spendthrift coming into possession of his inheritance, it has wasted that idealism in a year of civil war. We have to build up again in its place an idealism of labour and of thought and it is not asking much that the few hundreds a year necessary should be spent to begin what may grow to be a very important work of national scholarship, a work for which all the scholars of the world will be grateful, a work which will enhance the reputation of this country. I, therefore, propose the amendment in its amended form: "That a Committee of the Seanad be appointed to submit to the Government a scheme for the editing, indexing, and publishing of manuscripts in the Irish language now lying in the Royal Irish Academy, Trinity College and elsewhere; for the scientific investigation of the living dialects; for the compiling and publishing of an adequate dictionary of the older language; that the Committee have power to invite the assistance of persons not members of the Seanad, and to take evidence on the subject, the Committee to consist of four members of the Seanad." I am now able to add the names of four members, Senator MacLysaght, Senator Mrs. Green, Senator Mrs. Costello, and myself. I find it a little difficult to suggest a quorum because those members will add to their numbers persons—

AN CATHAOIRLEACH: I think you ought to be a little careful about that. . . . You are asking the Seanad to appoint a Committee which is not only to include Senators but outsiders, but that is not what your motion says.

MR. YEATS: You are quite right. It was really a question of getting assistance. The quorum ought to be two, I should think.* [I, 992-995]

Motion put and agreed to.

* Yeats was made chairman of the committee on the whole matter. He and Mrs. Stopford Green, assisted by various Irish scholars, prepared an elaborate report on the state of Irish studies, embodying numerous suggestions and schemes for extending the work of qualified scholars. The Senate passed the report unanimously, but the Dáil took no action on it, and has not to this day. (See pages 68-77 of the present volume for this report.)

12. THE LANE PICTURES

May 9, 1923. For a full description of this protracted and tangled controversy consult Our Irish Theatre *by Lady Gregory.*

MR. W. B. YEATS: I have the following motion to move:

"That the Seanad ask the Government to press upon the British Government the return to Dublin of the pictures mentioned in the unwitnessed codicil to Sir Hugh Lane's will."

This is an old question. We have been agitating now for some years, and I have some reason for saying that the opposition against the return of these pictures is dying away. I think the justice of our case has been generally admitted. It is simply a question of the inertia of Government and of giving them the necessary impulse towards arriving at some definite decision. It is necessary, however, I think, to remind you of the circumstances under which that codicil was written. A good many years ago now Sir Hugh Lane established in Dublin a famous gallery of modern pictures. When he established it there was no modern gallery here in which students could study, and they had to go abroad to do so. Sir Hugh Lane was no mere picture dealer, but, in the words of an eminent authority, he lifted the trade of picture dealer into the realm of art. He sold pictures merely that he might buy other pictures, and he bought pictures in order that he might endow a great gallery. After he made the Dublin Municipal Gallery the most important collection of French pictures outside Luxembourg, he was somewhat discourteously treated by some of the Dublin newspapers and certain persons, and an acrimonious controversy arose.

In 1913, under the impulse of that controversy, he made a will leaving certain pictures, generally known as the Hugh Lane French pictures, to the National Gallery of London. These pictures had been given to the Municipal Gallery conditional on certain requests being carried out. Those requests were not carried out, and he gave them to the English National Gallery. He felt the pictures were not valued here. He lent them to the English National Gallery to show that they were real pictures of worth. Then under irritation he made this will, by which he left all his property, with the exception of those French pictures, to the National Gallery of Ireland. He left certain pictures to the Municipal Gallery, but he left the French pictures to the London National Gallery. Two years later, in 1915, when he was going on a journey to America, which he knew to be dangerous, he made a codicil by which the National Gallery was to return the pictures known as the French Pictures back to Ireland. He wrote that codicil in ink. He signed it on each page. I have a photographic copy of it in my hand; when he made a slight correction in the date he initialled that correction. No document could be more formal except for one omission. He never had it witnessed. He spoke of this change of mind to various people. I have in this pamphlet three affidavits of how he spoke of changing his mind, and wishing that Ireland had his French pictures. Of his intention there can be no question whatever. From those various documents I think I may read you one affidavit made by his sister:

I, Ruth Shine, of Lindsey House, 100 Cheyne Walk, London, S. W., widow, do solemnly and sincerely declare as follows:

The late Sir Hugh Lane was a brother of mine, and he is hereinafter referred to as "my brother."

In January, 1915, my brother spoke to me of making another will. He went to Dublin, however, without having done so. It was there (on February 3rd) that he wrote and signed his codicil and locked it in his desk at the National Gallery in a sealed envelope addressed to me; it was very clearly and carefully written and I have no doubt whatever that he considered it legal.

My brother had no ordinary business habits in the ordinary sense of the word, and was ignorant of legal technicalities. He dictated both his wills to me, the first leaving all to the Modern Art Gallery in Dublin, and the second leaving all to the National Gallery of Dublin, with the exception of the French pictures left to London. But for my persistence, neither would have been witnessed; even when he dictated the second will he had forgotten all I had told him about that necessity. So little am I surprised at there being no witnesses to the codicil that my surprise is altogether that he should have written it so carefully. He must have made rough drafts, as he composed letters with great difficulty, and the codicil was so well written.

I think from my knowledge of him that if he thought of a witness at all he would perhaps have considered that a codicil to an already witnessed will needed no further formality. When he sealed up the envelope he was going on a dangerous journey to America, and was so much impressed by that danger that at first he had refused to go at all unless those who had invited him for business reasons would insure his life for £50,000 to clear his estate of certain liabilities, and he thought he was going not in seven or eight weeks, as it happened, but in two or three.

I have approached this subject without any bias in favour of Dublin, but as his sister, anxious that his intentions should be carried out, and I make this declaration conscientiously believing the same to be true and by virtue of the provisions of the statutory Declaration Act, 1835.

RUTH SHINE

Declared at Markham House, King's Road, Chelsea, in the county of London, this 13th day of February, 1917
Before me,
G. F. Wilkins
A Commissioner for oaths.

That codicil would have been legal in Scotland. It seems to us that a request made to a great Gallery is something different from a request made to an individual; that a great Gallery like this cannot desire to retain property which was left to it by accident, and that it must desire, as we do, the return of these pictures if they are set free by Act of Parliament legalizing the codicil. We believe that that Act of Parliament can be obtained. One Irish Chief Secretary had prepared such a

Bill, but it has been pushed aside by the pressure of Parliamentary business. It is very important for Ireland to recover these pictures. With the addition of the French pictures the Municipal Gallery is more than doubled in its importance, for those pictures are complementary to the pictures here in Dublin. He was not only a connoisseur; he had the gift of arranging pictures so as to display them to the best advantage. With those pictures there, we should have in the Municipal Gallery a possession which in future generations would draw people to Dublin, and help in enriching the city and the whole population by bringing those pilgrims. The actual money value of the pictures is hard to decide, because pictures constantly change their value, but about twelve years ago they were valued at about £75,000. It is quite probable they are worth more now. One picture, by Manet,* might be bought at £20,000. They also have this further importance: they will never be in the market again. The great pictures of that period in French art are already finding their way into national collections. It is precisely for that reason that certain English critics have tried to keep the pictures in England. They know that if they cannot keep these French pictures in London they can never have a representative collection of French art. In fighting to recover these pictures you are fighting for a unique possession which will always remain unique and always give prestige to the Gallery that contains it.** [I, 1037-41]

Motion put and agreed to.

* Conjectural. The text gives Malet.
** A second speech by Yeats on these matters appears on pages 118-124.

13. PAYMENT OF SENATORS

June 6, 1923. Payment of Members Bill. The monthly allowance for Senators was £30. Mr. MacLysaght's proposed amendment to the Payment of Members Bill was that the allowance should be withheld if a Senator did not attend at least half of the meetings of the Seanad, illness excepted.

MR. YEATS: I hope, when I have heard the arguments for and against Senator MacLysaght's proposal, that I shall be able to vote against it. It is one of these proposals which, without rousing in one any very strong conviction, does rouse in one a very strong distaste. I think it should only be proposed in this Seanad if there had been gross abuse. I think there has been no gross abuse. I think it can quite well be postponed for a considerable time. The proposer of it has said that the attendance has been very high.

MR. MACLYSAGHT: Fairly high.

MR. YEATS: He said that the average of attendance had been 60 per cent, and that is very high. Many Senators have attended at great loss to themselves, and some with danger to themselves.* This Seanad has

* A partial summary of property damages sustained in 1923 by Senators blacklisted by the I.R.A. will give point to Yeats's remarks:

Jan. 29: The Earl of Mayo's mansion in County Kildare burned. Of his great collection of paintings, only three Reynolds portraits escaped the fire.

Jan. 29: Sir Horace Plunkett's estate in County Dublin completely wrecked by land mines.

Feb. 1: Moore Hall (County Mayo), a famous work of architecture and one of the finest residences in Ireland, totally destroyed.

Feb. 1: Home of Senator Thomas Lineham (Corke) burned.

Feb. 4: Burning and looting of home of Dr. O'Sullivan.

Feb. 5: Dr. G. Sigerson forced to resign from the Senate because of threats to his very important library of Irish materials.

Feb. 19: Sir John Keane's mansion in County Wexford burned to the ground.

Feb. 22: Home of Countess Dowager of Desart in Killeny, one of the country's finest residences, burned down.

a brief but honourable career. If you are to create and preserve a habit of service you must trust that habit and you must be ready to prefer integrity to any kind of weight and measure. [I, 1121]

Motion defeated.

14. CENSORSHIP OF FILMS

June 7, 1923. Censorship of Films Bill: Report Stage. Mr. McKean proposed that "to protect the youth of the country," minors should not be permitted to go to cinemas unattended by adults.

MR. W. B. YEATS: I would like to comfort the mind of the Senator who has just spoken, but I am afraid I shall not succeed. This is really an old problem—a problem that has troubled a great many writers and a great many artists. I remember myself—

AN CATHAOIRLEACH: Are you rising to second this amendment?

MR. YEATS: I am not.

AN CATHAOIRLEACH: Senator McKean's amendment reads as follows:— "Young people under 16 years of age shall not be admitted to any cinema theatre unless in a body from their schools, and under the supervision of their masters." Does any Senator second that?

THE EARL OF WICKLOW: Not that I am in the smallest degree in

Feb. 23: Oliver Gogarty's West Ireland home, in County Connemara, totally burnt, with loss of many valuable modern paintings.

Feb. 26: Home of Senator the Earl of Granard, Castle Forbes ("one of the most magnificent inhabited castles in the British Isles"), ruined by land mines.

Mar. 9: Senator Sir Thomas Esmonde's home, a 1300-year-old building with modern (seventeenth-century) additions, containing many valuable furnishings, burnt.

The above list of damages is compiled from Donal O'Sullivan's *The Irish Free State and Its Senate* (London, 1945). This book is an indispensable work for anyone interested in the politics of the Irish Free State; it has saved me from many an error of fact and interpretation.

sympathy with the amendment which has been proposed, but in order that we shall not be deprived by our rules of the rest of Senator Yeats's remarks, I should like to be allowed to second the amendment.

MR. YEATS: A terrible responsibility has been thrust upon me. I merely rose to say that I thought I could comfort the mind of the Senator who proposed this amendment. Artists and writers for a very long time have been troubled at intervals by their work. I remember John Synge and myself both being considerably troubled when a man, who had drowned himself in the Liffey, was taken from the river. He had in his pocket a copy of Synge's play, "Riders to the Sea," which, you may remember, dealt with a drowned man. We know, of course, that Goethe was greatly troubled when a man was taken from the river, having drowned himself. The man had in his pocket a copy of "Werther," which is also about a man who had drowned himself. It has again and again cropped up in the world that the arts do appeal to our imitative faculties. We comfort ourselves in the way Goethe comforted himself, that there must have been other men saved from suicide by having read "Werther." We see only the evil effect, greatly exaggerated in the papers, of these rather inferior forms of art which we are now discussing, but we have no means of reducing to statistics their other effects. I think you can leave the arts, superior or inferior, to the general conscience of mankind. [I, 1147-48]

Amendment put and negatived.

15. NATIONAL HEALTH INSURANCE

June 25, 1923. National Health Insurance Bill.

MR. YEATS: I have neither the special knowledge nor the special aptitude to enable me to form a conviction on this subject, but I have a very strong conviction that legislation ought not to be hurried through the Seanad, unless it is absolutely necessary to do so. Bill after Bill has come up here, and we have been told that we have to legislate on each in a hurry. Very likely it was necessary to do so, but I hope that necessity will very seldom arise. When I came to-day I was told that there had been a debate on the subject, that the Dáil had thrown out the resolution, and that it had said various things, polite and otherwise, about ourselves. I tried to see a report of the debate. I found that one Senator had it, and he could only spare it long enough for me to read half through one speech. I was told that there were two other copies somewhere. I searched, and could not find these two copies anywhere. I was offered copies of several other debates, but not these two copies.

We are, therefore, in this position; we were talking on a resolution on which the Lower House has expressed what are, doubtless, well-informed opinions, and we know nothing about these opinions. If we decide in favour of our own original resolution, and against the other, we are acting discourteously—a discourtesy we cannot help. I, therefore, suggest that on this subject we are, I think, all unanimous, that we do not want any more legislation hurried through this House if it can possibly be helped. [I, 1308-1309]

16. LOCATION OF PARLIAMENT

July 11, 1923. Oireachtas [Irish Parliament] Accommodations.

MR. YEATS: I propose that that Committee [i.e., a joint committee of both houses to consider how suitable accommodations for Oireachtas may be obtained] be formed. I think that it should be clearly understood that in appointing this Committee, or in agreeing to sit upon it, we do not in any way commit ourselves to any decision about the site. I understand that plans are being prepared for Kilmainham,* but I think it must be understood that we are quite free to object to that site, even as a temporary site. I do not say that I would recommend that, but we must go into it quite freely. I think most of us have a feeling that it is undesirable that Kilmainham should be the permanent site of an Irish Parliament. People coming up from the country, we feel, will want to find themselves nearer the Parliament than they would be if you put it out into a remote suburb.

AN CATHAOIRLEACH: I think, Senator Yeats, it would be more convenient if you simply move the motion for the appointment of the Committee and then when their report comes up it will be open to the Seanad to deal with it as they think fit.

MR. YEATS: The only thing I would like to say is that the time is very short to report. I understand the reason for its urgency, but it is undoubtedly very short, and it may be necessary to take expert opinion. For instance, if we were going to the Royal Hospital temporarily, changes would be made in that building that would be of very great architectural importance, and it might be desirable for us to take expert opinion as to whether the permanent value of the building will be in any way affected by these designs. So I think that it will possibly be necessary for us to ask for an extension of time. [I, 1390]

17. INSPECTION OF PRISONS

July 26, 1923. Public Safety Bill (Occasional Powers): Second Reading.

MR. YEATS: I have no doubt that the Seanad will pass the Second Reading of this Bill. They have found the Government are very able and courageous, and they have come to us and said that these

* The large rambling county prison in the western suburb of Dublin, in which Parnell and other Irish patriots were confined.

powers are necessary, but I have little doubt that the Seanad will modify the details of the measure. I am myself interested in one detail. Before Christmas I went to President Cosgrave and I consulted him about the advisability of proposing a resolution in the Seanad asking for the inspection of prisons. He gave me what seemed at the moment sound reasons against my proposing it. About two months ago, or less, a very influential body of Senators went to the President and again proposed an inspection of the prisons. President Cosgrave gave that body reasons against the inspection which I did not think were so sound, and I do not think that many of us came away convinced. I am sorry that when this question arose in the Dáil that a resolution in favour of inspection of prisons was not passed there, especially as Mr. O'Higgins when speaking in the Dáil said that the Government would have no objection to the inspection of prisons if the Government appointed the inspectors. I do not think that any one of us would dispute the methods of appointment if we had able and independent men appointed, but I am sorry that no clause has been inserted in the Bill dealing with this, and I hope the Government will agree to it in the Committee Stage. In saying this I do not wish it to be supposed that I hold that any particular set of charges that have been made against the prisons are true. I have no doubt whatever of the gross exaggeration of these charges, but I am equally certain that no body of men could be trusted with a responsible power over any other body of men, especially if these men are their political opponents, and I think that some kind of independent inspection and independent appeal ought to be allowed. There are other questions I could touch upon, but I will reserve what I have to say to the Committee Stage. I only speak on this now because I would like the Government to consider whether or not they can meet us on that point. [I, 1440]

18. ANCIENT MONUMENTS

August 3, 1923. Land Bill: Report Stage.

MR. YEATS: In the absence of Sir Thomas Esmonde I desire to move the following amendment:—To insert before Section 46 a new Section as follows:—

The definition of ancient monuments contained in Section 14 of the Irish Land Act of 1903 shall include any monument which in the opinion of the Land Commission is of archaeological interest and shall where the Land Commission so declares also include the site for the monument and such portion of the land adjoining it as is necessary to prevent injury and afford access.

I think it will be unnecessary for me to waste the time of the Seanad in dealing with the subject. I had something to do with the insertion of a somewhat similar clause in the Land Act of 1903. I understand now that the Inspector of the Land Commission himself reports on these monuments, and I hope the Government will see that he does so thoroughly, for I know cases where admirable monuments have not been inspected. [I, 2129]

19. SIR HORACE PLUNKETT

November 14, 1923. Resignation of Sir Horace Plunkett (largely the result of intimidation by Irregulars).

MR. W. B. YEATS: If I am in order, I wish to say how much the whole Seanad regrets Sir Horace Plunkett's resignation. I understand that the establishment of every technical school and agricultural college in this country is the result of his efforts, and we know that the methods of organization which he perfected in Ireland have spread to a good many countries. In Ireland he organized, I think, 180,000 farmers into his organization. If I remember rightly the last public letter of President Roosevelt, when he was President of the United States, was a letter of thanks to Sir Horace Plunkett for his great services to the organization of agriculture in the United States. We, here, forget sometimes how great his work has been and how much honourable fame it has brought to this country. [II, 65]

20. THE IRISH LANGUAGE

November 14 1923.

MR. CUMMINS: I wish to move the following resolution: "That the Prayer be read in Irish and English every day." I think the time devoted to Irish in the Seanad, even though it is only half a minute a day, will produce valuable results.

THE EARL OF MAYO: I beg to second the motion.

MR. YEATS: I wish to make a very emphatic protest against the histrionics which have crept into the whole Gaelic movement. People pretend to know a thing that they do not know and which they have not the smallest intention of ever learning. It seems to me to be discreditable and undesirable. I hope this will not be taken as being unsympathetic to the Gaelic movement. In the Abbey Theatre, on Monday night, a play in Irish was produced, and the theatre was packed with an enthusiastic audience. They knew Irish, and they were able to understand the language of the play, but I think this method of histrionics and going through a childish performance of something we do not know, and which we do not intend to learn, will ultimately lead to a reaction against the language. I wish to say that I wish to see the country Irish speaking. [II, 89-90]

21. CIVIL SERVICE

January 15, 1924. Civil Service Regulation (No. 2). Amendment: to open posts for civil service personnel reciprocally among the nations of the British Commonwealth and Ireland. Opposed with the argument that "all the great people have gone abroad. . . . let us keep our people at home. . . ."

MR. YEATS: I think it is an insult to the national pride that this country should be asked to accept gifts from Canada while it refuses to give anything in return. It is, I think, an insult to the country to suggest that it is to be kept up by law and artificial barriers. The last Senator has described how in various parts of the world he found Irishmen occupying most important positions. These Irishmen should be able to occupy them at home without the law making a barrier to put them into them. If we do not pass this amendment we will have a precedent in this country for keeping out the experts from abroad whom we require and putting into position the ignoramuses at home whom we would be glad to lose. We will constantly have to import able men to teach this country many things that Irishmen had no possibility of acquiring. Every country in the position of this nation at the beginning of its career, has to import talent. You are now to create a barrier which will make it impossible to do so, and, with the insulting theory that good intellects at home require protection. It is only the bad intellects at home that require protection, and I hope they will never get it. [II, 369-70]

Amendment lost.

22. THE IRISH LANGUAGE

January 15, 1924. Civil Service Regulations (No. 2). There was marked resistance to adding the words "or Civic Guard" after the Irish words "Garda Siochana" in the Regulation.

MR. YEATS: The question troubles me very much. If I am attacked by a footpad and wish for protection how can I call for that protection by using words that I cannot pronounce? [II, 383]

23. BRITISH EMPIRE EXHIBITION

January 15, 1924. Sir Thomas Esmonde moved "that with a view to encouraging Irish Industry steps should be taken for the Representation of the Irish Free State at the forthcoming British Empire Exhibition."

MR. YEATS: There is a certain body interested in artists, of which I am Chairman, and we had this matter before us at the last meeting, and there was exactly the same difference of opinion there as we find here now. We found out that invitations from the exhibition reached various artists at the end of last September to send in their work. We have been carrying on some correspondence with Ministers to find out whether the work of Irish artists would be classified with the general mass of English artists and other artists from different parts of the Empire, or whether they would be treated separately, and exhibited in a different room. I do not know whether we have had any satisfactory answer yet. It is possible it is too late to have them separated in a separate room, and that they would go along with others from different parts of the Empire under the head of "British Artists." If they went into a separate room we would have very distinct possibility for Ireland.* About 16 years ago Sir Hugh Lane gave an exhibition of Irish Art in London, and it was discovered that some of the most famous artists were Irish. If our artists now had not the opportunity of exhibiting separately they would be driven back in the public estimation. At the same time we were not sure but it might be too late now to organise a separate Irish art section, and to bring into it men like Orpen and Lavery and Shannon, and if we could not recover these men we would have an Irish section that would not fully represent us. I am very much in favour of having Ireland represented at an Empire exhibition, but I am very anxious that the representation should be adequate, and I confess that I have not before me any facts upon which I could feel assured upon that subject. [II, 398]

24. INSPECTION OF PRISONS

January 23, 1924. Public Safety—Powers of Arrest and Detention Bill.

MR. YEATS: When this Bill was before the Seanad in its first form some months ago one of the Labour Members got a clause inserted providing for the inspection of prisons, camps and other places. I had something to do with the endeavour to get that clause inserted, but, as far as I know, it has never been acted upon. The clause is one "Providing for the inspection of such prisons, camps and other places, and the visiting of persons detained therein, by responsible persons, to be appointed by the Minister." I have felt for some months considerable curiosity as to the fate of that clause, and I think our Labour Senators have also felt some curiosity. I shall be very glad if that curiosity could be satisfied, to know whether these persons have been appointed, whether they have inspected the prisons; and if they have not been appointed, if they are going to be appointed, and when. [II, 489]

* The sentence so reads in Seanad Eireann Report, but is obviously missing a clause.

25. INDEPENDENCE OF JUDGES

February 6, 1924. Courts of Justice Bill, 1923: Third Stage.

MR. W. B. YEATS: I have not spoken hitherto on this Bill though I have voted in favour of the amendment of Senator Brown. What I rise for is to point out, to the President, a point of view which has occurred to me. Some of us so far from being hostile to the Government are deeply influenced by sympathy for the Government. We feel it has acted with great courage and justice in difficult times. We are scrupulously anxious to put aside our question of sympathy in favour of the question of judging these amendments. We want to judge these amendments in an abstract way, in the light of history, keeping in mind the fact that all civilized Governments that we know of, have found it necessary to insure the independence of the Judges from the Executive. It is difficult for us to press that point because we have felt that the Government have no desire to influence the decision of the judges. There is a feeling in this country among a number of people—it may be an unjust feeling—that the judges have hitherto been subservient to an alien Executive. Some members of this House have gone to the other end of the balance and thought that they would secure safety by being quite sure that an Irish Executive would have considerable control over judges. Those who take my point of view have done their best to secure that the Irish Judges shall be independent of every Executive whatsoever. [II, 714-15]

26. THE NATIONAL GALLERY

March 19, 1924. Ministers and Secretaries Bill: Third Stage.

MR. W. B. YEATS: I am troubled by one statement. The only matter in this Bill that interests me very much is the National Gallery and the Museum. I understand from the Attorney-General that if the Government has no policy for any particular Department it will not keep it within the purview of the Executive Council, or within the purview of Ministers within the Executive Council. If, therefore, the Government has no policy with regard to the National Gallery or the Museum, will it hand them over to the Minister for Fisheries to be administered by him, or by the Minister for Agriculture, as they were before, or by the Postmaster-General? [II, 1089]

27. QUESTIONING THE GOVERNMENT

March 19, 1924. Ministers and Secretaries Bill: Third Stage. Yeats replies to the Earl of Mayo's proposal that it should be possible to question representatives of departments freely and that written answers to such questions should be obligatory.

MR. YEATS: I feel that if we have conferred upon us this very embarrassing privilege of questioning the Government, as each one of us is supposed to have the entire of Ireland as his constituency—I suffer in my postage already—I think the burden of my daily post, of all our daily post, will be entirely intolerable. I hope, therefore, that the Government will absolutely refuse to answer any questions on anything whatsoever. [II, 1106]

28. NATIONAL GALLERY AND ART SCHOOL

April 3, 1924. Ministers and Secretaries Bill: Fifth Stage.

DR. W. B. YEATS: With the indulgence of the Seanad I would like to say certain things that, properly speaking, I should have said on the Second Reading, but which I did not say for reasons which I will explain presently. At various periods during the last six months some persons interested in the National Gallery and the School of Art urged upon Ministers the desirability of placing the Museum, the National Gallery and the School of Art under the Ministry of Education. When this Bill came to the Seanad I saw with great satisfaction that these institutions were placed under the ministry of education. After the Second Reading I read the Bill with more attention, and I found that the Government possesses the right to transfer any particular institution to any particular ministry it likes. That fills me with alarm. It is, no doubt, quite right that the Government should have such power, but I will take this opportunity of saying that I hope the Government will not transfer these particular institutions to any ministry except the Ministry of Education, without consulting these bodies.

A number of us went on a deputation to one of the Ministers about five months ago. I have been trying to remember for the last half hour what Minister. I think it was the Minister for Industry and Commerce, but I cannot remember. The deputation laid before the Minister a very strong case, I think, to have these institutions included under the Ministry of Education. I would like to touch lightly on that now, because if the Government decide to transfer these institutions to some other branch nothing will be done but to lay on the table of the Seanad certain papers announcing the fact. I may be away and may not see them, and other members of these bodies may know nothing about the matter. It is very important for the future industrial prosperity of this country that Art teaching should be brought in relationship to industry. That can only be done by some unified system of teaching which will include such institutions as the School of Art and the schools of the country. In the newer universities in Germany and in Scandinavia they have professors of the arts for purely industrial reasons. They have found it essential in order to hold their own in the manufactory of the world that they should teach certain principles of good taste in order that their various forms of manufacture may possess good taste.

I begin with an example of what I hope may happen in this country. I understand that the Ministry of Education will form in the immediate future a Technical Board. One of the things that might very well come before that technical board for consideration is the lace industry of Ireland. If you go back a few years you will find that Ireland had an exceedingly prosperous lace industry, which employed a large number of people. That lace industry has lost its market to a very great extent, partly through the hasty production of good old designs—the rough and ready manufacture at a quick rate of good old designs—and partly through the equally hasty production of exceedingly bad modern designs. For instance, I understand that in some cases 3s. 6d. would be given for a design to some student. That is about the same amount as the Free State Government thinks it necessary, I understand, to give for a design for a postage stamp. It would be possible for the Technical Board of the Ministry of Education to obtain from Austria or Sweden a teacher of lacemaking, one with the highest possible accomplishments in the art, so that the industry might be restored to prosperity. Such a teacher would be employed in two ways, going to the country to inspect, and teaching at the School of Art. You have another example of the effect of teaching in the School of Art on the industries of this country. About twenty years ago, and I had a little to do with it, a teacher of stained glass was brought from England and employed in the Dublin School of Art. That teacher was brought chiefly through the efforts of Miss Purser. The manufacture of stained glass in Ireland was then the worst in the world. Now, some of the very best stained glass in the world is made here. One of the makers of the worst stained glass in the world twenty years ago was a man named Clarke. The maker of some of the best stained glass in the world today is his son. These are unusual topics to raise in the Seanad.

AN CATHAOIRLEACH: I was about to intervene and say that myself, although I am very loth to curtail you as you are very interesting. What has this to do with the Ministers and Secretaries Bill?

DR. YEATS: I want the Government to keep Art teaching under the Ministry of Education in order that a unified system of Art teaching may arise in this country associated with education, so as to help manufacturers. The deputation to the minister was told that the argument against having the art institutions under the Ministry of Education was that they might be subordinate to a purely mechanical system of teaching, and thereby suffer as art institutions—I think that is very unlikely under the present Minister. That argument was put strongly. I beg the Government if they detach these institutions from the Ministry of Education, not to give them to any other ministry, but to give them a ministry of their own. The Arts in Ireland have suffered for several generations from having been under the Department of Agriculture. The Department of Agriculture had no policy in connection with them except a deadly one. When Sir Hugh Lane, for instance, was rejected when he applied for the position of head of the Museum in Dublin— the one great connoisseur we had—he was rejected on grounds which had nothing whatever to do with the Arts, but which were simply matters of policy of that Department. When the Department was remonstrated with, an official used this argument: "The time has not come to encourage the Arts in Ireland." If you place these particular institutions under any ministry except the Ministry of Education or under a ministry of their own, you will find that the time has not come to encourage the Arts in Ireland. [II, 1316-19]

29. LOCATION OF PARLIAMENT

May 1, 1924. Temporary Accommodation of Oireachtas: Report.

MR. W. B. YEATS: Senator Jameson said in the course of his speech that the great stones were being taken down from the Four Courts. If that is true, there may be some explanation of it. It is possible that the building is unsafe, and so on, but it is a matter so serious that I think, as the stones are being taken down, the Government should give some explanation to the public. We have there a building of great importance and great dignity, which we ought to have looked upon as a trust received from the past. It has been, unfortunately, almost destroyed, although not absolutely, I think, beyond the possibility of rebuilding, and I think we should preserve what remains of it. I desire to support what Senator Jameson has said.

The explanation of the curious position in which we find ourselves is that the majority of the Dáil think that the only thing for them to do is to go into Leinster House, but they think it would be an unlucky decision to make for themselves; and the Government would like to go to Kilmainham, but they think that it would be an unlucky decision to make for themselves, and both bodies of men are trying to get somebody else to make the decision. I read in Fraser's *Golden Bough* that there was a certain nation of antiquity which once a year used to launch a model ship and sail out into the ocean and put on board all the reluctant community. If we do not do that we must make a deposit of the ill-luck of the community. The Joint Committee of both Houses has been appointed to act in the capacity of that model ship and carry away that ill-luck from the majority of the Dáil and the government. I hope at this moment the Chairman is trying to exercise his ingenuity in framing a resolution to defeat that object. [III, 55-56]

30. AGAINST OVERHASTY LEGISLATION

May 21, 1924. Future Business (Overhasty Legislation).

MR. YEATS: I wish to support one part of Senator Brown's speech. This House should remain sitting after the 4th July. There are certain Bills of pressing importance to this country. It is important we should not create a precedent of hasty legislation. If we create that precedent it will last long after our time, but there is an immediate necessity for certain Bills. I am only speaking to draw the attention of the Government to the fact that no Bill has been introduced on copyright. I would like to draw the attention of the President to the fact that the copyright of certain Irish dramatists in America is being lost because there is no copyright act to enable the registration of those copyrights in Washington. I would, therefore, urge this House to remain sitting until we have passed the necessary legislation in order that the Government may find, when it meets in October, that our work has been done. [III, 131]

31. THE NATIONAL MUSEUM

June 4, 1924.

DR. YEATS: If the Government decides to remain in this building for a few years have we not means of getting expert opinion on the question as to whether these buildings are properly secured against fire? I do not think we ought to take the opinion of a board which is under the influence of the Government. If, as a result of the Seanad staying here there was a fire, and the Irish gold ornaments and other national treasures were destroyed, it would be a final touch to the evil reputation of this nation. Certainly, I do not think that the Seanad could throw off responsibility on the question. If we are to be kept here we should have expert opinion, independent of the Government and the Board of Works, as to whether these buildings are properly protected against fire.

AN CATHAOIRLEACH: We have this apology, we are kept here against our will.

DR. YEATS: If we are going to be kept here cannot some other place be found to contain the national treasures. [III, 195]

32. IRISH MANUSCRIPTS

June 4, 1924. Final Report of Committee on Irish Manuscripts.

DR. YEATS: I beg to move the adoption of the final Report* of Committee on Irish Manuscripts as follows:

This Committee was appointed by Resolution of the Seanad adopted on the 19th April, 1923, in the following terms:

That a Committee of the Seanad be appointed to submit to the Government a scheme for the editing, indexing, and publishing of manuscripts in the Irish language, now lying in the Royal Irish Academy, Trinity College, and elsewhere; for the scientific investigation of the living dialects; for the compiling and publishing of an adequate dictionary of the older language. That the Committee have power to invite the assistance of persons not members of the Seanad and to take evidence on the subject; the Committee to consist of Senators W. B. Yeats, Mrs. Alice Stopford Green, Mrs. Costello, and Edward Maclysaght; two to form a quorum.

The Committee met in accordance with this Resolution on 26th

* This report was written by Yeats and Mrs. Stopford Green.

April, 1st May, 3rd May, 31st May and 27th June, 1923, and on the 21st of May, 1924.

Evidence was heard from the following witnesses:—Dr. R. L. Praegar, Dr. R. I. Best, The Rev. Dr. Lawlor, Dr. Douglas Hyde, Mr. E. J. Gwynn, F.T.C.D.; Professor O'Bergin, Professor T. O'Rahilly, Mr. R. Foley, and Professor Tomas O'Maille.

It was decided to make the following report to the Seanad:

Your Committee is gravely impressed by the responsibility now laid upon the Saorstat towards the Irish people. For the first time in many centuries our country, free and independent, is charged with the pious duty of preserving and making accessible to Irishmen the mass of learning and tradition which forms the basis of our National history— a body of manuscript tradition bequeathed to us by a noble succession of scholars and scribes throughout a thousand years of labour, and further enriched by folk-lore, folk-song and music and the important study of topography.

It is well known that the British Government by its political and administrative policy through a long course of centuries did in fact make wreckage of Irish learning and language. But we are bound to remember that in our own time among the rulers there were men who did not remain deaf to claims of scholarship. We may recall the valuable services rendered from time to time by enlightened statesmen in funds allotted to such work as the Irish volumes of the "Rolls Series"; the "Historical Manuscripts Commission"; the "Ancient Laws of Ireland"; published by the Government under the direction of the Commissioners; the "Ulster Annals," which it published under direction of the Royal Irish Academy. The Government was prepared to do the same with the "Annals of Tigernach," when unfortunately, the editor recommended died. A grant in aid to the Academy was employed, to issue the Todd Lectures, Facsimiles, etc., etc. For some years a grant was also given to the School of Irish Learning founded by Dr. Kuno Meyer, £700 in all.

These are a few illustrations of obligations to the country recognised by a British Administration. We claim that the Irish Nation should fare no worse under a home Government, when it depends on its own honour, its own patriotism and resources, to complete the task of research, to preserve for future generations all that has been or can be saved of older learning, and to secure to the people of Ireland their full national tradition.

We may observe that the present moment is unusually favourable for reviving and enlarging the study of Old Irish Law and government even beyond the bounds of this country; since the important research work of Professor MacNeill is rousing amongst foremost Continental scholars a new interest not only in questions of language but of the study of Comparative Law. By judicious use of its scholars and its means Ireland may take the lead in a new historic movement.

Your Committee, in the course of enquiry, has interviewed many witnesses of the most diverse groups and opinions. We have endeavoured to find out the points on which there is practically unanimous opinion, and to advise measures which are of urgent necessity, and promise useful results under conditions of sound administration and sympathetic aid. We therefore recommend the following suggestions as a basis for any scheme of financial assistance:—

(1) The editing and publishing of important texts, both of the early and the classical periods and of modern times, considering Irish literature as forming one indivisible whole. This work would involve grants in aid of publication to competent scholars.

(2) Publication of photographic facsimiles of important Codexes by the latest scientific processes. This is most essential for purposes of study. A grant to aid in the production of such a facsimile might be given to a learned body outside Ireland—for example, to the Oxford Press for the publication of Ms. Laud 610.

(3) The dictionary of Old Irish in course of preparation by the Royal Irish Academy under the editorship of Dr. Bergin—a work of enormous labour and difficulty—should receive further aid. Its progress must be slow, as the meaning and use of old Irish words can only be determined when more texts are made available by editors and photographers for

the work of the Dictionary. At present three workers are employed, necessarily on half-time which is as much as the excessive strain of the task will allow. The number of workers might be increased to six—all on half-time.

(4) The publication of Catalogues of MSS. is of great importance for students. Catalogues should be compiled not only for the Royal Irish Academy but for collections elsewhere as for example, in the Franciscan Convent, and the King's Inns, the National Library, and many others in Ireland or outside. We suggest that the Dictionary workers, and others, now employed at half-time, might most profitably also serve in this task of cataloguing.

(5) Investigation of living dialects. This work is of immense importance when dialects are rapidly dying out. It has been done in patches of the Irish speaking regions, but a systematic study is in fact essential, and the work cannot be relegated to volunteers. Research should be endowed. For example, a grant to a trained phonetist would be of the utmost value, with aid in the publication of his results. It is unnecessary to add how great would be the stimulus given by such training to local workers in Gaelic-speaking regions.

(6) Folk-lore, songs and traditions cannot be neglected. The best aid would be a grant towards publications of work done, as for example, a grant to the Irish Folk-Song Society in aid of publishing work submitted by the Society and approved.

(7) The Academy has drawn attention to two other needs of a pressing character: a survey of the antiquities of the country, such as is at present being carried out by Commissions in England, Wales and Scotland. In this connection it remarks that the measurements and plans of earthworks of different types and surveys of cairns already published by the Academy would serve as a nucleus for this undertaking. The work might be very gradually carried out, district by district.

Excavations should also be conducted under scientific direction of the more important archaeological sites, to determine their age, significance and historical associations.

In the view of the Committee all grants should be allocated by an authoritative body, including trained Irish scholars, animated with the desire to encourage students by the assurance of means of publication of their work. We have, therefore, enquired into the best machinery by which these suggestions may profitably be carried out, and the body to which public funds should be entrusted.

The body which in our opinion is marked out for the development of Irish studies is the "Royal Irish Academy," which has now incorporated the "School of Irish Learning."

The Academy was founded to encourage learning in a wide range of Sciences in which it has earned distinction. It has also charge of linguistics and archaeology, and Irish research has long been a notable part of its business. Since it has no special funds for archaeological work, apart from occasional grants, its resources have been spent on publication. The Government grant is £1,600, and £885 comes from members' subscriptions and other sources. On a total income of £2,485—with establishment charges of £1,050—the Academy shows an admirable record of careful administration. It must be remembered that the benefits it contributes to Irish learning include a library rich in Irish books, to which the public have admission; a valuable collection of ancient MSS; and also the printing in its "Proceedings" of important Irish communications. For many years past an average of six hundred pounds —over a third of its annual income available for general publication— has been expended on Irish subjects, literature, archaeology and the like. At the moment the Leabhar na hUidhre (Book of the Dun Cow) is being published at a cost of about £1,000. The task of publishing the Irish Dictionary, now calculated at nearly £600 a year, must necessarily occupy many years, and remain a heavy charge on finances. All strictly Irish work of the Academy is delegated to an "Irish Studies Committee," drawn from two older groups—the Dictionary Committee and the Irish Manuscripts Committee. It has enlisted in its service all the best Irish scholars, whose knowledge, experience, and ardour in the cause cannot be surpassed.

The "School of Irish Learning" was founded in 1903 by Dr. Kuno

Meyer at a time when there was no regular teaching in Dublin of an advanced nature in Old or Middle Irish. The School held summer courses by Professors invited to lecture from England, Scotland, Germany, Denmark, and Norway, and students were attracted from overseas by the remarkable training thus offered. Travelling scholarships were also given by the School with excellent results. With a single exception all the professors and lecturers in Irish in the National University Colleges have been students of the School, as also have been Professors of Celtic in Great Britain and abroad. The work of the School has for some years past been limited to summer courses, the last of which, in 1923, was a remarkable course in Phonetics, and the study of a living Irish dialect by Professor Sommerfelt, of Christiania.

An important and enduring work of the School was its journal *Eriu,* devoted to Irish philology and literature, and recognized in the learned world as the leading review of its kind. The School also published text-books on Old and Modern Irish which are now used by scholars in every country.

It was felt desirable at this time to unite forces working for Irish scholarship, so as to avoid all overlapping of effort, all conceivable competition in publications, and all unnecessary doubling of rent and services. An amicable arrangement has, therefore, been made by which the School of Irish Learning has been incorporated in the Academy, and so far as Irish studies are concerned, *Eriu* remains the common Journal, the representative work of the united body.

Your Committee, therefore, after careful consideration, recommend that the authoritative financial control of any grant allotted by the Government should be placed in the Academy whose Irish Committee is fully qualified, trained in this special work, generous in outlook, and easy of access to all.

We believe that additional funds allotted to it by the Government will be spent not only with a due sense of stewardship, but with an earnest desire to advance the cause of Irish Learning, and to complete the national work of restoring to the Irish people their inherited tradition both of ancient and of later times.

We fully realize the overwhelming claims on the Government in these times. On the other hand we feel it to be of great importance that some earnest should at once be given of its sympathy with the national desire to renew and broaden its historical tradition and faith. We, therefore, recommend that an additional annual grant be given to the Academy, and especially earmarked for the disposal of the Committee of Irish studies on the lines indicated in this Report. In the existing state of our national finances we do not name a definite sum, but we urge that as liberal a grant as possible should be given immediately, and that the Government should bear in mind that as soon as our financial position allows not less than £5,000 per annum should be devoted to Irish research.

> (Signhithe),
>
> W. B. YEATS, Cathaoirleach an Choiste (Chairman of the Committee).
>
> EIBHLIN BEAN MAC COISDEALBHA.
>
> A. S. GREENE.
>
> EAMON MAC GIOLLAIASACHTA.

I hope and indeed I have no doubt that the Seanad will accept this report. I would like, however, to draw the special attention of one section in the Seanad to the nature of the report. Certain members of the Seanad have, I think, a great dislike to pray in a language they do not understand. There are other members of the Seanad who dislike having our Acts of Parliament expensively printed in two languages. That may be right or wrong, but this is an entirely different question. We are asking the Seanad to urge upon the Government to do a work for learning, a work for literature and a work for history which any Government in the world would consider its duty and its privilege. This country possesses a great mass of old mediaeval literature in the Irish language. There are great collections of manuscripts in the Royal Irish Academy, in the Library of Trinity College, at Maynooth, and in the Franciscan library. There are very large collections of manuscripts in other countries. There is a great collection in the British Museum, in the Bodlean [*sic*], and in the Louvain. These manuscripts are a historical trust to this nation, but they should be interpreted, edited, indexed, and catalogued.

Much work has been done on them in the past—much by Irishmen, much by Germans, and to some extent we may say that the centre of Irish scholarship has in recent years been in Germany. But the German interest is only primarily a philological interest. If we are to exhaust the value of these manuscripts for literature and history we must do that work ourselves. They possess first of all their value to this country; then they possess their value to the world. They consist of stories, annals, and poetry. I think that all the famous stories have been translated and have been edited. We will learn nothing new of importance about Finn and Cuchulain and other old Irish heroes or Kings of the legendary period. The annals have to a great extent been edited and translated, but I understand, they have been badly edited and translated in many cases, and if they are to be of historical value that work has to be done over again. In the case of poetry there is probably still a large quantity of untranslated and of even unread poetry.

That poetry would be of two kinds: First of all, what is called the official poetry, not of great literary value but of great historical value—the work of the official Bards. But there is also much poetry which is personal expression—that kind of poetry which Dr. Kuno Meyer has translated in recent years. If we can judge the unread and unedited by the read and edited, they will be of supreme value. I should say that we had evidence given before us, that great scholars might work for 100 years on the old Irish manuscripts now in the possession of the nation, and in the possession of other nations without having exhausted the subject. We are anxious that provision should be made for that work and that the work should be carried out. Already the traditional imagination in these old books has had a powerful effect upon the life, and

I may say upon the politics, of Ireland. People forget that the twenties, forties and fifties of the last century was the forming period of Irish nationality, and that the work was begun by O'Donovan, Petrie and men steeped in this old literature.

We owe it also to learning and the scholarship of the world that we should provide means for the doing of this great work. Twenty years ago, in Paris, I knew slightly the great French scholar, D'Arbois de Jubainville, who devoted his life to the study of our literature because he believed that only through that literature could he find light on the most important secular event in human history. Going back 1,000 or 1,200 years before Christ we find Dorian tribes descending on the Mediterranean civilization. They destroyed much and wandered much, and it has been held that we owe to their destruction, the story of the Fall of Troy, and to their wandering, the Story of Odyssey. D'Arbois de Jubainville considered that only through Irish literature can you rediscover the civilization of these tribes before they entered the Mediterranean. That does not mean that our people were the Greeks or that our literature is as old as 1,200 years before Christ, but our legends and our books have preserved and gathered together the old literature and much of the history of a similar period. We ask you to urge upon the Government that they shall place in the hands of the Royal Irish Academy sufficient funds. We heard much evidence and we came to the conclusion that the Royal Irish Academy itself contains within its limits practically all the great Irish scholars and that it is the proper body to carry out this work in a spirit of scholarship. The danger is that it may be carried out in some other spirit. It is most important that nothing should be taken into consideration except the interest of scholarship alone.

It should not be allowed to become a means by which some man will make a living until he gets some other occupation; the money should be used to help a man whose life-work is study and scholarship. It has been contended that the Royal Irish Academy is not a democratic body and that therefore we should not ask the Government to endow it in this way. I have heard it contended that it is not a democratic body because by its rules it can only elect seven new members every year. Twenty years ago I should not have been able to invite you, with the same confidence, to ask the Royal Irish Academy to undertake this work, because twenty years ago it had not that rule. It could elect any person who professed himself interested in the subjects with which it dealt. That rule of electing only seven members a year was instituted in order to raise the position of the Academy by making it necessary to elect those only who were eminent in the studies of the Academy, and not merely interested in those studies. I think I am right in saying that since that rule was passed the Academy has risen more and more in the estimation of the learned, and in helping it to do its work we are helping a body which has advanced the learning of this country. I beg to move the adoption of the Report.* [III, 161-171]

33. THE NATIONAL MUSEUM

June 19, 1924. Temporary Accommodation of the Oireachtas.

MRS. WYSE POWER: I move:—

That the Second Report of the Joint Committee on the temporary accommodation of the Oireachtas be received and adopted.

COLONEL MOORE: I second the motion.

AN CATHAOIRLEACH: The matter is now open for discussion.

DR. W. B. YEATS: I move:—

That the consideration of this report be postponed for a fortnight.

* After discussion, the Report was adopted by the Senate; the Government, however, failed to concur, and has not to this day, though certain folk lore and other literary societies in Ireland have since adopted many of the recommendations of the Report.

I do this because it recommends that the Parliament should remain in the present building. We are very anxious to have some investigation made as to whether the Museum is safe from fire, and I do not think we can very well consider the matter until we have had some investigation. Some of us are going, in the course of a few minutes, to see the Minister on the question, and I think it may be desirable to have a Special Committee of this House appointed to take expert advice. I do not see how we can come to any conclusion on the question at all until we can have some evidence before us as to the security or otherwise of the national treasures. I, therefore, move that the consideration of the Report be postponed for a fortnight.

> *After considerable discussion, mainly concurring in Yeats's motion, he continued:*

DR. W. B. YEATS: I simply want to say, as a matter of explanation, that I have brought forward this resolution with no other object whatever, except to find out whether the collections are or are not in danger from fire or otherwise from our residence here. I have not done this in the interest of the Royal Dublin Society or because of preference for any particular site. But I do think we have got to find out, and the responsibility is ours individually, whether our residence here is causing danger to the national collections. I think the Chairman has made our case in telling us that it was not raised until a few weeks ago, in other words that it was not considered by the Committee.

Another question I would like to have asked the Board of Works as to the protection against fire is, whether they had to improve this protection at the instance of Senator Mrs. Green's agitation. Had they to have more protection or to improve it, because if they improved it, then the former protections were inadequate, and the Board of Works are in the dock. I see every reason for postponing this matter until we get expert opinion. I am only asking for postponement, not rejection of the report. It is quite possible that when we have heard this opinion we will decide that this is the best place. [III, 260-72]

> *After discussion the motion was agreed to.*

34. THE IRISH LANGUAGE

July 2, 1924. It was proposed that railway tickets, signs, and notices should all be printed in English and Irish "to have the language in evidence."

DR. W. B. YEATS: The last time I spoke in the Seanad was on a question connected with Gaelic. It was to bring before the Seanad a report of a committee that had been dealing with Gaelic studies. I asked the Seanad to support a proposal by which the Government would be asked to give £5,000 for the endowment of Gaelic. Senator Colonel Moore tells me that he hopes to get the Government to endow Gaelic. If such a proposal comes before the Seanad, I will certainly support it. I ask the Seanad to throw out this amendment. I do so in the interests of the sincerity of Irish intellect, and not in the interests of those who pretend that they know a language that they do not know.

MR. MACLYSAGHT: I did not say that you know Irish.

DR. YEATS: I have tried to learn it. When you put up, as this amendment proposes, a notice telling a man where he is to cross a railway line, you put it up to give him the best practical information. That is the only thing you have to consider. To put that up in the Irish language is to create a form of insincerity that is injurious to the general intellect and thought of this country and to create an irritation against the Gaelic language. That causes a general irritation against all Irish thought, all Irish feeling, and all Irish propaganda. That is a cause of irritation that is increasing daily in this country, I am sorry to say. If the Gaelic League or any other Irish national interest is injured it will be injured by an attempt to force Irish on those who do not want it. Endow creation by scholarship, and press that on the Government, but do not set up a pretense of people knowing a language that they do not know by perpetually printing, and in other ways, exhibiting something in the Irish language.

COLONEL MOORE: Senator Yeats has made a rather impassioned speech on this subject.

DR. YEATS: I want the Senator to know that all the passion is not on one side. [III, 526-30]

After further discussion the amendment was withdrawn.

35. THE STAINED GLASS INDUSTRY

July 3, 1924. Finance Bill, 1924: Second Stage.

DR. YEATS: I am not competent to give an opinion on the great issue of Protection versus Free Trade. The Government, however, is engaged in certain experimental measures, and that justifies me in bringing before them one particular industry in this country. When the Fiscal Committee was meeting, various persons engaged in the making of stained glass brought before them a proposal that they should get Protection. I shall deal in a moment with the argument why they need that protection. I think the Fiscal Committee, or certainly some of its members, were exceedingly sympathetic towards that proposal, but as the Committee decided to report in favour of Free Trade they were unable to put anything in the Report on the subject. The position of the stained-glass industry in Ireland is this: It is purchasing now some of the very best glass in the world and it has been faced for some years past, except one short interval, with the competition of the most inferior stained-glass which is produced in Germany for Irish use, especially produced for the bad taste of Ireland. It is impossible that our stained-glass can compete against the mass production of Europe. Under no circumstances whatever can it do so, because an artist producing fine glass cannot supervise more than a very limited number of assistants. The moment you increase those assistants beyond a certain point, the quality of that glass and the design deteriorates. You cannot get the same qualities of colour. The mass manufacture of glass will always be inferior. There was a short period during the war when our Irish stained-glass had not to face that competition. They at once found an exceedingly fine market at home, and it was the finding of that exceedingly fine market which helped them to establish themselves in their great artistic pre-eminence as creators of that beautiful glass. Then, with the Armistice came the old competition of Germany in a much worse form, but owing to the depreciation of the German coinage, the Germans were able to import their glass much cheaper than ever before.

I do not ask the Government to put on such a tariff as would exclude German glass produced under these circumstances. They would have to put on an absolutely prohibitive tariff, probably 300 per cent., but I would ask the Government to consider the advisability of putting a tax of say 50 per cent. on German glass, until the money market becomes normal between England, Ireland and Germany. Nobody connected with the production of glass in Ireland desires to have a tax against English glass. I think I am right in saying that there is not one person in Ireland connected with the making of glass that desires such a tax. The reason of that is that they are artists, not manufacturers. They recognize that Ireland and England are now producing the best glass in the world, and that it would be an unfair thing for Ireland to seek an economic advantage against English glass. They believe that it would be to the advantage of this country, and its reputation, if the Government were to protect it against the very inferior quality and products of other countries that are made to be consumed in this country and this country only. It requires a firm Government to say certain things are fine and certain things are not fine and should not be encouraged. The Government has shown great courage in many ways and I suggest it should show enough courage to support what is fine in the arts. [III, 615-17]

36. THE NATIONAL MUSEUM

July 16, 1924. Temporary Accommodation of the Oireachtas. Motion to move to Leinster House to prevent hazard of fire to National Museum.

MR. W. B. YEATS: My interest in this question is almost entirely confined to seeing that the contents of the Museum are safe. I do not know whether the members of the Dáil or all the Senators realize that practically no Museum is insured, that the contents of Museums are so valuable that money cannot replace these articles. The National Gallery in London, the great museum in South Kensington, and the British Museum or the Irish Museum are not insured. You must, therefore, see to the safety of the Museum in the way that you do not see to the safety of any ordinary building. Furthermore, you cannot trust merely to your fire-extinguishing apparatus—though in museums that is generally of the most perfect kind—because the waterhose may do as much injury as the fire to the Museum. There is only one thing that you can do with the museum, and that is to see to it that no fire can break out in it. Certain precautions are taken all over the world. In no museum in the world is smoking permitted. Now here we have a refreshment room where there is cooking. In Museums where there is a refreshment room they are specially constructed on concrete floors, so that fire cannot break out. Furthermore, all these museums of any importance are detached buildings. About twenty years ago it was discovered that the National Gallery in London had an inflammable building up against it. There was great agitation in England, and there was great indignation, and that building was pulled down. In the Bodleian Library which I know very well—I used it for several years—artificial light is not permitted, because it is an old inflammable building, though not more inflammable than our building. These are the ordinary precautions taken all over the world for the protection of national treasures. Are we going to be less civilized than any other country?

Some few weeks ago the various persons whose business it was to look after these treasures memorialised the Government in various forms. The Royal Irish Academy laid weighty evidence before the Government to show that the national treasures were not safe. The Visitors to the Museums, who are persons appointed under Act of Parliament to take care of the treasures there, laid a memorial before the Government, showing that the National treasures were not safe. A petition was laid before the Government signed by bishops, peers, representatives of all the learned institutions of Ireland, and some twenty Senators of this house, stating that the national treasures were not safe. The answer to that was the statement by the Government that they were safe. Then, some three weeks ago we postponed the report of the Special Committee that we might see the technical evidence upon which the Government had stated that the national treasures were safe. I have here on the Table, where it should have been laid by the Government, the report of the technical advisers. It was sent to the Clerk of this House that members might see it. I will read you one extract from the letter, written on the 22nd June by the Board of Works to the President's Secretary:

"We beg to report that the danger of fire to the National Museum is undoubtedly increased by the fact that the Seanad and its officials are housed there, and that the Senators and officials are accustomed to smoke on the premises. It is also true that the annexes of the Museum at present used as refreshment rooms and kitchen are lined with wood, and are very inflammable, and that there is a wooden hut near the annex, occupied by soldiers, which also is of an inflammable nature."

And yet we are told the national treasures are safe! The Board of Works might have said more. They might have pointed out that the floors are of wood, that the centre of danger—the kitchen and the bar —are flanked by rooms containing highly inflammable material. Any of you can go and look at the place next the dining-room and you will find a room packed with inflammable show-cases. If you go into the passage in the same building you will find bottles full of spirits—not the spirits they have in the bar, but spirits of another form equally dangerous in case of fire. Then the Board of Works, in this letter which I have here, go on to say: "Special precautions have been and are being taken to meet these risks." They define their precautions. They are putting up a fireproof door between the passage and these buildings. They are putting up a fireproof door between the building on that side and the other Museum. They are putting up a further fireproof door above the way that leads down to the spirit stove, which is under the kitchen. Then they go on to say that there are other precautions. There is, they say, a fireproof door outside the room upstairs where the gold ornaments are housed. There is no fireproof door there. There is a burglar-proof door.

They say an inspector goes round every night and that that is the best precaution of all. If that is the best precaution of all, I think very badly of the others. If that man does his work properly, it will take him at least an hour to see after the library which he is to inspect, and to see that all the windows there are properly shut. I am informed that it would take him several hours to make his rounds, if he does his work properly. A fire might therefore have a very considerable start before he discovered its existence. And that is the best precaution according to the Board of Works! Then, why were not those precautions taken months and months ago? Can we trust anything the Board of Works says to us when we have it that it is only now it takes such precautions. Is it a fitting guardian of the public treasures? The only thing it does, as a result of Mrs. Green's agitation, is to put up those fire-proof doors. If the Oireachtas remains here, there is only one thing to be done if the Museum is to be safe—that is to rebuild the kitchen and those other apartments somewhere else. The chief danger is from those buildings.

I cannot imagine that the Government desires to take less precaution in guarding its national treasures than Governments do in other countries. I can only think that the situation has arisen because of the extraordinary apathy of this country—an apathy that has come upon everything in connection with the national life in the recent past. I cannot imagine that if the mind of this country were what it was seven or eight years ago, the people would think for a moment of leaving in any greater danger their treasures than the treasures, say, in South Kensington Museum or the British Museum. These treasures are the only visible signs we have that we ever had a civilization. I do not think that the Government, if they gave thought to the matter, would like to set such an example before the people of this country of contempt of things of the mind. They are bringing in an ambitious Education Bill. They talk occasionally of their desire to see this an able, intellectual country. But if they are going to pay less respect than any other country does to their national treasures, to the irreplaceable things, who in this country will take them seriously when they speak of their desire to see this country able and educated? [III, 876-80]

Motion put and declared carried.

37. THE NATIONAL MUSEUM

July 16, 1924.

MR. YEATS: I beg to move:—

That the Seanad is of opinion that for the purpose of satisfying the public mind as to the sufficiency of the safeguards provided against fire in the National Museum and the adjoining buildings, the Government should obtain a detailed report from an independent expert; and that inasmuch as Sir Edwin Lutyens will be in Dublin by invitation of the Tailteann Games Committee in August, he should be requested to make the report.

I do not think that the Board of Works would object to an independent expert being asked to give an opinion on this matter. I find in one of their statements this occurs: "If the Government were to ask to make a special inquiry into the matter, it would be desirable to agree to do so, and to appoint a committee for the purpose, as the report of such a committee would probably have more weight than Departmental representations." That statement of the Board of Works admits on principle the desirability of there being some outside report upon the question. I was in London until last night, when I returned for this meeting, and while there I inquired from various persons whose business was the safety of museums from fire, and I was told that Sir Edwin Lutyens would be the right person to examine into the question and to make an expert report. I went to him and asked him if he was invited by the Government to make a report, would he do so, and he said he certainly would. He will be in Dublin on August 1st as the guest of the nation. I think he would be regarded as the most acceptable person to do this. There is no one connected with architecture in the world who is a higher authority or whose word or opinion would be more universally accepted. [III, 881-82]

Motion put and agreed to.

38. NORTHERN IRELAND

October 17, 1924. Motion: "That this Senate is of opinion that the interests of the country as a whole would be best served by an agreed solution of outstanding problems affecting the relations between The Irish Free State and Northern Ireland."

MR. FARREN: . . . We have got to assert our manhood and set aside all this kind of humbug and nonsense about goodwill and toleration for people who will not have toleration, and who will not meet us in a spirit of goodwill. The more you endeavour to placate the people responsible for trouble in the North of Ireland, the more will they be prepared to kick you. The only one Ulsterman I ever knew was James Connolly, and he told me that you could never placate those people. The only way you will ever get them to have goodwill or to understand the situation is by standing up to them and letting them have all they want. I do not want civil war, and I am not anxious for fighting. Neither do I want cant or humbug, and, therefore, I will oppose the resolution and vote against it.

MR. YEATS: I do not think the Senator who has just spoken fully understands the resolution. We are not asking the Government to withdraw from the Commission* and we are not asking that the Commission should come to an end. We perfectly understand the Government's promise to those people. The Government promised those people the Treaty and they are bound to give the people of this country the Treaty; they cannot give anything else but the Treaty. What the resolution suggests is that before the Commission has reported, President Cosgrave, without giving anything away whatever, should make another appeal to the North to meet him in counsel. He is surrendering nothing. I think we quite recognise that nothing will probably come out of that appeal of President Cosgrave. To some extent we have to think of the future: we have to think of educating the next generation.

Results of a very evil kind may happen from the report of the Commission no matter what way it reports, and it is exceedingly important that no responsibility for those results should lie with the Government of the Free State. I have no hope of seeing Ireland united in my time, or of seeing Ulster won in my time; but I believe it will be won in the end, and not because we fight it, but because we govern this country well. We can do that, if I may be permitted as an artist and writer to say so, by creating a system of culture which will represent the whole of this country and which will draw the imagination of the young towards it.

Now, I have spoken very seriously, but I want to turn from serious-

* Commission to study problems relating to the boundary between Northern and Southern Ireland.

ness to a fact which has been burning in my imagination since this meeting began—a discovery I made which has lightened this serious subject for me. I have been looking for a historical precedent for the remarkable fact that certain Englishmen who afterwards became Cabinet Ministers and in other ways rose to the highest positions in the State went over to Ulster about 15 years ago and armed the people at a time of entire peace and urged them, and are now urging them, to use these arms against us. I have found a historical precedent which establishes that it is an old custom of the British Government. I have found that Edmund Burke in the middle of the eighteenth century drew attention to a very remarkable item in the Estimates of the year. It was an item of so much money for the purchase of five gross of scalping knives, which scalping knives were intended to be given to the American Indians that they might scalp the French. [III, 1060-61]

After further discussion, motion put and carried.

39. HISTORIC MONUMENTS

June 10, 1925. Shannon Electricity Bill. It was proposed that whenever any monument of antiquarian interest was to be disturbed in the course of the electricity scheme, the Board of Public Works should be notified.

DR. YEATS: There are many monuments which we should respect and which will become of great importance to this country, not only to the education of our own people, but to the tourists who come here. Therefore, they will be of financial value. There is a famous poem called "Clonmacnoise," which will be sung by the people of other countries. A poem of the late Mr. Rolleston is so beautiful that it will in all probability bring many tourists into that district if you can protect the ruins:

"In a quiet, watered land, a land of roses
Stands St. Kieran's city fair,
And the warriors of Erin, in their famous
                              generations,
Slumber there."

I think I am the first person who has quoted a poem in the Seanad. I only do so because I am sure the poem will be, to use the appropriate words, "a definite asset."

> *One clause in the proposed amendment read: the Minister shall "with the consent of the owner of the land on which the monument stands" make an order for its preservation.*

COL. MOORE: I am not satisfied with the Minister's statement. It has to be done with the consent of the owner. I remember a few years ago when a certain person owned Tara, and certain people came over from England and they said the Ark of the Covenant was at Tara. They proceeded to dig up the whole place. There were protests from a great many people, some of them friends of mine. Arthur Griffith went there and protested, but it was no use. The farmer said he was paid to do it, and he intended to do it. There was much damage done to Tara. I would like something to be done in the case of unreasonable men of that kind, and so prevent them from destroying ancient monuments.

DR. YEATS: We stopped that man. I was on that expedition. [III, 418-20]

40. DEBATE ON DIVORCE

June 11, 1925. In February, 1925, the Dáil requested the Committee on Standing Orders to frame an Order which would make it impossible for any person to introduce a bill of divorce a vinculo matrimonii. *When this motion was sent to the Senate the chairman, Lord Glenavy, ruled it out of order because it appeared to be an attempt to legislate by resolu-*

tion. On June 11 the Senate considered the Committee's report and passed a resolution that a Standing Order be framed by which Bills of Divorce must receive a first reading in each House before being proceeded with in the Senate. This would provide facilities for any person to promote a bill of divorce carrying the right to remarry; the Dáil could kill any such bill by refusing to give it a first reading. In any case, of course, the overwhelming Catholic majority in the Dáil and Senate would have made passage of a private Bill of Divorce virtually an impossibility.

AN CATHAOIRLEACH: The next item on the Order Paper is "Report of the Joint Committee on Standing Orders (Private Business) on the position in Saorstát Eireann of Bills relating to matrimonial matters (consideration resumed)." There is a motion in regard to this matter standing in the name of Senator Douglas.

> *Senator Douglas had moved that a message be sent to the Dáil requesting that it concur with the Senate in the Resolution that private Bills of Divorce "must be read a first time in each House before they are further proceeded with in the Senate."*

DR. YEATS: Before Senator Douglas speaks, I would like to say that some of us desire to discuss this question on its merits, and I would like to know whether it would be in order to do so before he proposes his resolution.

AN CATHAOIRLEACH: I hope that every Senator will discuss the motion on its merits, but I think what you want to get an opinion from me on is whether you can discuss the main question as to whether there should be divorce *a vinculo matrimonii*.

DR. YEATS: Yes.

AN CATHAOIRLEACH: That undoubtedly does arise on the report and motion, and I shall not stop a general discussion upon it if that is the wish of the House.

DR. YEATS: Owing to Senator Douglas's motion, I shall have to move its rejection in order to make the discussion germane to the matter.

AN CATHAOIRLEACH: That will give you an opportunity of enlarging on the matter.

DR. YEATS: It goes against my heart.

After a discussion by several Senators of certain technical matters, the Chairman returned to the topic of divorce legislation as follows:

AN CATHAOIRLEACH: The House might like to spend the rest of the day over this divorce business and if that is the universal wish of the House, the debate might be resumed. I call upon Senator Yeats.*

DR. YEATS: I speak on this question after long hesitation and with a good deal of anxiety, but it is sometimes one's duty to come down to absolute fundamentals for the sake of the education of the people. I have no doubt whatever that there will be no divorce in this country for some time. I do not expect to influence a vote in this House. I am not speaking to this House. It is the custom of those who do address the House to speak sometimes to the Reporters.

COLONEL MOORE: No, no.

AN CATHAOIRLEACH: Perhaps the Senator would please address me. I do not think that Senator Yeats intended to be uncomplimentary to the House, but his observation looked like it.

DR. YEATS: I did not intend to be uncomplimentary. I should have said I do not intend to speak merely to the House. I have no doubt whatever, if circumstances were a little different, a very easy solution would be found for this whole difficulty. I judge from conversations that I have had with various persons that many would welcome a very simple solution, namely, that the Catholic members should remain absent when a Bill of Divorce was brought before the House that concerned Protestants and non-Catholics only, and that it would be left to the Protestant members or some committee appointed by those Protestant members, to be dealt with. I think it would be the first instinct of the members of both Houses to adopt some such solution and it is obvious, I think, that from every point of view of national policy and national reputation that would be a wise policy.

* Yeats's speech could not have come as a surprise to many of the Senators as he had already published his notes for an earlier version of his speech in George Russell's (A.E.'s) paper *The Irish Statesman*, March 4, 1925. (See Appendix II.)

It is perhaps the deepest political passion with this nation that North and South be united into one nation. If it ever comes that North and South unite, the North will not give up any liberty which she already possesses under her constitution. You will then have to grant to another people what you refuse to grant to those within your borders. If you show that this country, Southern Ireland, is going to be governed by Catholic ideas and by Catholic ideas alone, you will never get the North. You will create an impassable barrier between South and North, and you will pass more and more Catholic laws, while the North will, gradually, assimilate its divorce and other laws to those of England. You will put a wedge into the midst of this nation. I do not think this House has ever made a more serious decision than the decision which, I believe, it is about to make on this question. You will not get the North if you impose on the minority what the minority consider to be oppressive legislation. I have no doubt whatever that in the next few years the minority will make it perfectly plain that it does consider it exceedingly oppressive legislation to deprive it of rights which it has held since the seventeenth century. These rights were won by the labours of John Milton and other great men, and won after strife, which is a famous part of the history of the Protestant people.

There is a reason why this country did not act upon what was its first impulse, and why this House and the Dáil did not act on their first impulse. Some of you may probably know that when the Committee was set up to draw up the Constitution of the Free State, it was urged to incorporate in the constitution the indissolubility of marriage and refused to do so. That was the expression of the political mind of Ireland. You are now urged to act on the advice of men who do not express the political mind, but who express the religious mind. I admit it must be exceedingly difficult for members of this House to resist the pressure that has been brought upon them. In the long warfare of this country with England the Catholic clergy took the side of the people, and owing to that they possess here an influence that they do not possess anywhere else in Europe. It is difficult for you, and I am sure it is difficult for Senator Mrs. Wyse-Power, stalwart fighter as she is—

MRS. WYSE-POWER: I do not see why my name should be mentioned.

AN CATHAOIRLEACH: It is not in order to refer in this way to members of this House.

DR. YEATS: I am sure it is difficult for members of this House to resist the advice of Archbishop O'Donnell.

MR. FITZGERALD: I think this is becoming very heated.

DR. YEATS: We shall all be much bitterer before we are finished with this question.

AN CATHAOIRLEACH: Order, order; address the chair.

MR. FARREN: Is it in order for a Senator to be bringing in names?

AN CATHAOIRLEACH: I am not a judge of taste. I cannot rule on matters of taste and I cannot say it is out of order.

DR. YEATS: Addressing the Catholic Truth Society in October last he used these words:

"No power on earth can break the marriage bond until death . . . that is true of all baptised persons no matter what the denomination may be. To be sure we hear that a section of our fellow-countrymen favour divorces. Well, with nothing but respect and sympathy for all our neighbours, we have to say that we place the marriages of such people higher than they do themselves. Their marriages are unbreakable before God and we cannot disobey God by helping break them."

That is to say that you are to legislate on purely theological grounds and you are to force your theology upon persons who are not of your religion. It is not a question of finding it legally difficult or impossible to grant to a minority what the majority does not wish for itself. You are to insist upon members of the Church of Ireland or members of no church taking a certain view of Biblical criticism, or of the authority of the text upon which that criticism is exercised, a view that they notoriously do not take. If you legislate upon such grounds there is no reason why you should stop there. There is no reason why you should not forbid civil marriages altogether seeing that civil marriage is not marriage in the eyes of the Church—

MR. IRWIN: Is it in order for a Senator to read his speech?*

AN CATHAOIRLEACH: It is not in order precisely, but very great latitude has been allowed always in regard to that. In fact, when dealing with a complicated question of this kind personally I think sometimes an advantage is derived from Senators sticking to their text. They are more likely to do that if they are reading from documents. I am bound to say in defense of the particular Senator that he is only reading, now and then, when quoting.

MR. O'FARRELL: I think you, sir, might appeal to Senators to restrain their feelings even though they may not agree with what is said. We do not agree with it, but that is no reason why we should lose our heads.

AN CATHAOIRLEACH: Particularly so in the case of a distinguished Irishman like Senator Yeats.

DR. YEATS: These are topics on which it is desirable that the use of words should be carefully weighed beforehand. That must be my excuse. It is just as much adultery according to that view as the remarriage of divorced persons is. Nor do I see why you should stop at that, for we teach in our schools and universities and print in our books many things which the Catholic Church does not approve of. Once you attempt legislation on religious grounds you open the way for every kind of intolerance and for every kind of religious persecution. I am not certain that there are not people in this country who would not urge you on to that course. I have nothing but respect for Most Rev. Dr. O'Donnell. I am told that he is a vigorous and able man, and I can say this for the speech from which I quoted, that if unwise in substance it was courteous in form. But what have I to say of the following extract from an article by Father Peter Finlay:—

"The refusal to legalise divorce is no denial of justice to any section of our people; it is no infringement of the fullest civil and religious liberty which

* Owing to his defective eyesight, Yeats could not glance at his notes, but had to bring them directly to his right eye, which gave the impression of reading from his text.

our Constitution guarantees to all. As well say that prohibition of suttee is a denial of justice to the Hindu widow. The Hindu widow had a far clearer right to do herself to death on her husband's funeral pyre—her religion imposed it upon her as a duty—than any member of a Christian community can have to put away his wife and enter into a state of public legalised adultery. England acted justly, and in fulfillment of a plain and grave moral obligation, when she forbade suttee in India. The Irish Free State will act justly, and in fulfillment of a plain and grave moral obligation, in refusing to legalise absolute divorce and re-marriage among ourselves."

In a previous part of the essay he compares divorce with polygamy, robbery, and murder. I know little or nothing about Father Finlay's career. It may have been eminent and distinguished, but I am sure that very few members of this House will think with pleasure of following the guidance of a man who speaks with such monstrous discourtesy of a practise which has been adopted by the most civilized nations of the modern world—by Germany, England, America, France and Scandinavian countries. He must know that by every kind of statistics, by every standard except the narrowest, that those nations, because they so greatly exceed us in works, exceed us in virtue. Father Peter Finlay has been supported by an ecclesiastic of the Church of Ireland, the Bishop of Meath, who has even excelled him in invective. Perceiving, no doubt, that indissoluble marriage, which for the guilty party at least, he passionately desires, has in other countries made men and women exceedingly tolerant of certain forms of sexual immorality, he declares that every erring husband or erring wife should be treated as a robber, a forger, or a murderer. Now, there is one great difference between Father Finlay in his relation to this House and the Bishop of Meath. I think that Father Finlay may influence votes in this House, but I am sure that the Bishop of Meath has not influenced one. What is more, if the entire Protestant episcopacy in Ireland came out with a declaration on this subject, it would not influence a vote in this House. It is one of the glories of the Church in which I was born that we have put our Bishops in their places in discussions requiring legislation. Even in those discussions involving legislation on matters of religion they count only according to their individual intelligence and knowledge. The rights of divorce, and many other rights, were won by the Protestant communities in the teeth of the most bitter opposition from their clergy. The living, changing, advancing human mind, sooner or later refuses to accept this legislation from men who base their ideas on the interpretation of doubtful texts in the Gospels. It is necessary to say, and I say it without fear of contradiction, that there is not a scholar of eminence in Europe today who considers that the Gospels are, in the strict sense of the words, historical documents. Their importance is devotional, not historical. For any ecclesiastic to advise statesmen to base legislation on a passage that may lack historical validity, is to appeal to the ignorance of the people. I am sure that the majority of those who favour the indissolubility of marriage, are under the impression that it preserves sexual morality in the country that adopts it. I think that before they are entirely certain on that point, they should study the morality of countries where marriage is indissoluble—Spain, Italy, and the South American nations. We are not proposing to take from those nations our economics, our agricultural or technical instruction, but we are proposing to take from them our marriage laws. Before doing so, I think it would be well to make some study of the effect of the marriage laws on those nations. I have gone to the authorities available, and I find that, on the whole, they have successfully suppressed much evidence of immorality. There are no reports in the newspapers of divorce proceedings. The usual number of children are born in wedlock, but I do find there is a great uncertainty as to the parentage of these children, but then, public opinion discourages curiosity on that subject, and it is a habit to discourage any inquiry into the emotional relations of men and women. Among modern communities there is a demand* for happiness, which increases with education, and men and women who are held together

* *Seanad Eireann* gives "relations of men and women among modern communities. This is a demand," etc. The version I have given is from Yeats's corrected copy of the Debate.

against their will and reason soon cease to recognise any duty to one another.

You are going to have indissoluble marriage, but you are going to permit separation. You cannot help yourself there. You are going to permit young people who cannot live together, because of some intolerable wrong, to separate. You are going to invite men and women in the prime of life to accept for the rest of their existence the law of the cloisters. Do you think you are going to succeed in what the entire of Europe has failed to do for the last 2,000 years? Are you going to impose the law of the cloister on those young people? If not, you are not going to raise the morality of this country by indissoluble marriage. A great English judge, speaking out of the immensity of his experience, said that there is no cause of irregular sexual relations so potent as separation without the possibility of remarriage.

This is a question which I know to be exciting a good deal of interest. I know something of the opinions of those who will make the next generation in this country. I know it, perhaps, better than most of the members of this House, and I am going to give those young people, speaking from here, a piece of advice, though they are, perhaps, of a far less excitable temperament than I am. I urge them not to be unduly excited. There is no use quarrelling with icebergs in warm water. These questions will solve themselves. Father Peter Finlay and the Bishop of Meath will have their brief victory, but we can leave them to it.

I have said that this is a tolerant country, yet, remembering that we have in our principal streets certain monuments, I feel it necessary to say that it would be wiser if I had said this country is hesitating.

I have no doubt whatever that, when the iceberg melts it will become an exceedingly tolerant country. The monuments are on the whole encouraging. I am thinking of O'Connell, Parnell, and Nelson. We never had any trouble about O'Connell. It was said about O'Connell, in his own day, that you could not throw a stick over a workhouse

wall without hitting one of his children,* but he believed in the
indissolubility of marriage, and when he died his heart was very
properly preserved in Rome. I am not quite sure whether it was in a
bronze or marble urn, but it is there, and I have no doubt the art of
that urn was as bad as the other art of the period. We had a good
deal of trouble about Parnell when he married a woman who became
thereby Mrs. Parnell.

AN CATHAOIRLEACH: Do you not think we might leave the dead alone?

DR. YEATS: I am passing on. I would hate to leave the dead alone.
When that happened, I can remember the Irish Catholic Bishops coming
out with a declaration that he had thereby doubled his offense. That
is, fundamentally, the difference between us. In the opinion of every
Irish Protestant gentleman in this country he did what was essential
as a man of honour. Now you are going to make that essential act
impossible and thereby affront an important minority of your countrymen. I am anxious to draw the attention of the Bishop of Meath to
Nelson. There is a proposal to remove Nelson because he interferes
with the traffic. Now, I would suggest to the Protestant Bishop of
Meath that he should advocate the removal of Nelson on strictly moral
grounds. We will then have the whole thing out, and discover whether
the English people who teach the history of Nelson to their children,
and hold it before the country as a patriotic ideal, or the Bishop of
Meath represent, on the whole, public opinion. The Bishop of
Meath would not, like his predecessors in Ireland eighty years ago,
have given Nelson a pillar. He would have preferred to give him a
gallows, because Nelson should have been either hanged or trans-
ported. I think I have not greatly wronged the dead in suggesting
that we have in our midst three very salutary objects of meditation
which may, perhaps, make us a little more tolerant.

I wish to close more seriously; this is a matter of very great seriousness.

* The sting in this expression is the word "workhouse," which means a house for the
unemployed, or unemployable. Yeats's poem "The Three Monuments," written a couple
of years later, develops the sentiments expressed in this paragraph.

I think it is tragic that within three years of this country gaining its independence we should be discussing a measure which a minority of this nation considers to be grossly oppressive. I am proud to consider myself a typical man of that minority. We against whom you have done this thing are no petty people. We are one of the great stocks of Europe. We are the people of Burke; we are the people of Grattan; we are the people of Swift, the people of Emmet, the people of Parnell. We have created the most of the modern literature of this country. We have created the best of its political intelligence. Yet I do not altogether regret what has happened. I shall be able to find out, if not I, my children will be able to find out whether we have lost our stamina or not. You have defined our position and given us a popular following. If we have not lost our stamina then your victory will be brief, and your defeat final, and when it comes this nation may be transformed.

AN CATHAOIRLEACH: I have been looking through this report.* . . . So far as I can see it is purely a historical document. It does not make any recommendation and does not come to any conclusion. . . . I do not see that the House commits itself in any way either for or against the doctrine by adopting this report. . . . I only throw this out in order, if possible, to prevent this debate degenerating into an acrimonious discussion upon the question itself when the report we are considering is a rather colorless document.

MR. FARREN: Is it not rather late to discover that?

AN CATHAOIRLEACH: The discovery has been made and I am stating the facts.

MR. FARREN: One side of the case has been put. I cannot sit here any longer when you allow one person to put one side of the case. I insist on the other side being put.

---

* Donal O'Sullivan notes that Lord Glenavy had acquired the habit, during his long and brilliant career at the bar, of entering court with his brief unread and grasping the whole case, down to its details, in a few moments. On this occasion he had been reading the Report for the first time while Yeats was speaking.

AN CATHAOIRLEACH: It is quite disorderly and unfair for you to say that. Please sit down. I do not think the observation about insisting is quite correct.

MR. FARREN: I must protest against—

AN CATAOIRLEACH: Sit down; you are not in order. . . . I am not going to stop the debate. I have no power to do that, now that it has been opened in the way Senator Yeats opened it. . . .

COL. MOORE: The day is very hot and the Senator who spoke got very hot in mind and body. We saw the sweat falling down as he issued those splendid phrases for which he is famous. I wish he had not taken an absolute sectarian view of this matter. . . . The Senator has indulged in a diatribe about bishops of all sorts and politicians of all kinds. He has invented a lot of crimes which he said they committed . . . and made a series of statements which are not in any way true. He says that Protestantism stands . . . I will not say for liberty, but for this question of divorce. Let us see whether that is true or not. Before the Reformation there was no such thing as divorce. . . . In the last days of Elizabeth an Act was passed by the English parliament (the 44th of Elizabeth) all of whom were Protestant . . . absolutely prohibiting divorce. . . . He stated in the sixteenth century—

DR. YEATS: The seventeenth century.

COL. MOORE: The Senator says now the seventeenth century. In the next one hundred years, from 1600 to 1700, there were only five cases of divorce. . . . He quotes the poet, Milton, as an authority. I do not know whether the poet Milton ever wrote on divorce.

DR. YEATS: One of the most famous of all the prose works of Milton is on divorce, which the Senator should have been taught at school.

COL. MOORE: Anyway, the poet did not divorce his wife. His wife died.

AN CATHAOIRLEACH: We cannot turn this into a question as to what happened to the wife of John Milton.

MR. O'FARRELL: Appoint a Commission.*

* Yeats had a reputation in the Senate for calling for the formation of committees whenever a point appeared dubious.

COL. MOORE: Very well, we have heard a great deal about that and now—

AN CATHAOIRLEACH: Have we not heard enough? You have killed the lady.

COL. MOORE: I suppose I must let pass a great deal that the last Senator said although, indeed, it deserves much attention both from the position of the Senator himself and the eloquent speech he made. I have listened to the Senator's speeches in various places. He is an eloquent speaker, and the speech just spoken is equal to any I have ever heard. I think it is rather hard that we should not be allowed to give any sort of answer to him.

AN CATHAOIRLEACH: I have not stopped you at all.

COL. MOORE: Well, I do not want to go into it now.

AN CATHAOIRLEACH: Then do not complain of the hardship because I am not imposing it on you.

COL. MOORE: Very well . . . Young people now get married knowing quite well the marriage will only last a year.

DR. YEATS: An ancient Irish form of marriage.

COL. MOORE: What is the result? It leads to all sorts of lies and disrepute. . . . why not adopt the American method and say "I will give a divorce to any two people who come before me. Let anybody who wants a divorce have it."

DR. YEATS: I find, with regret, that I have, apparently, used the word "pressure," and am understood to mean that pressure was brought to bear on individual members. "Pressure" was not the word I wished to use, and it was not the word I had in my manuscript. It was hastily spoken. What I had in my mind was the effect of the Press, the effect of sermons, and the effect of all the letters that have been written on the feeling in this country, perfectly legitimate pressure. I had to give my speech what members thought was a religious turn, because it seemed to me that the only argument that I had to meet was a purely religious argument. I have seen no discussion in the Press and heard no discussion in this country which was not a purely religious argument, and it would be pure hypocrisy to deal with it on other grounds.

COL. MOORE: I had hoped the Senator would have dropped the religious argument. He changed it, but he has raised it again now.

DR. YEATS: I do not mean that pressure was brought to bear on individual members, but that arguments were used in the Press of the country—

MR. BENNETT: On a point of order, has Senator Yeats moved any motion, or is he entitled to speak a second time?

DR. YEATS: I am particularly unfortunate—

AN CATHAOIRLEACH: He has spoken previously on the motion for the adoption of the report. He is speaking now on Senator Douglas's motion, which is a different matter. I have allowed him to speak so far by way of explanation, but I must immediately ask him to direct his attention to Senator Douglas's motion. The Senator is quite at liberty to make any explanation, if he thinks he has been misunderstood, but when he has done that I must ask him to pass on to Senator Douglas's motion.

DR. YEATS: I can only speak on Senator Douglas's motion by addressing myself to the general question and I have no right to speak on the general question a second time. By way of explanation, however, I may say that I did not intend my speech to be an attack on the three great men whose statues are in our principal thoroughfare. It is probably the innate immorality of my mind that was at fault. I do not think that the memories of these great men of genius were swept away by their sexual immoralities. I still regard them as men of genius who conferred great gifts on their country. They do not cease to be men of genius because of these irregularities. To explain the extreme immorality of my mind a little further, I do not think there is any statesman in Europe who would not have gladly accepted the immorality of the renaissance if he could be assured of his country possessing the genius of the renaissance. Genius has its virtue, and it is only a small blot on its escutcheon if it is sexually irregular. [V, 434-80 *passim*]

SECOND TRIENNIAL PERIOD

December 6, 1925—December 5, 1928

At the first triennial election in 1925, seventy-six candidates stood for nineteen Senate vacancies. This unwieldy slate, together with an electoral process that favored group-supported candidates, had the effect of lowering appreciably the quality of Senate personnel. Nevertheless, the work of the Senate during the second period remains a remarkable record of devotion and industry: between 1925 and 1927 the Senate drafted three hundred legislative amendments, all but two of which were agreed to by an increasingly hostile lower House.

The principal matters before the government during the second triennial period reflect Ireland's sudden emergence from the straits of reconstruction into modern nationhood. Bills now fell into three main categories: (a) internal economy—taxation, agriculture, forestry, industrial development, commercial regulations; (b) external affairs—foreign trade, protection, relations with Northern Ireland, etc.; (c) cultural matters—the national school system, literary and artistic copyright laws, the designing of a new Irish coinage, etc.

For reasons of health, Yeats was present at Senate meetings less frequently now than in the earlier period. His speeches, however, grew only more vigorous and hard-headed, studded with valuable remarks on Ireland's cultural life, how it might be fostered and developed, how it was related to the general political and social life of the nation. He had become an eloquent and forceful speaker, as his addresses on Literary Copyright, The Lane Pictures, and Irish Education amply testify; and the articles he wrote concurrently on these and kindred topics (see the appendices to this volume) display a unique combination of practicality and vision.

41. WOMEN IN CIVIL SERVICE

December 17, 1925. Civil Service Regulation (Amendment) Bill, 1925. On discrimination as to sex in civil service appointments.

DR. YEATS: I think perhaps it would assist us if the Minister, before the discussion goes any further, would tell us if there is any objection to scheduling the posts for which women are not eligible to stand. I think it is essential that a Government in the position of our Government should not only be in the right, but should be obviously in the right, particularly as we are after a very anarchic period, and as we have an old legacy of suspicion. The Minister said one of the objections to appointing women to certain posts is that they may get married. I wonder if that is so? My only experience of the matter has been gained in the theatre, and I have not noticed that when an actress gets married she retires from the stage. No doubt the Minister may in many cases be right, but there is the danger of making it difficult for women to marry and discouraging marriage if there is any undue discrimination against women on the ground that they will withdraw from the Service on marriage.

As I have been listening to the Minister, I have been reminded of an essay which I read in my youth by Huxley. I think he called it "Black and White." In that essay he pointed out that women did possess certain physical disabilities. They were liable to be withdrawn from service owing to certain things—child-bearing, and so on. He made one point, that it was essential that no Government should, in any way by its laws, increase these disabilities. That should be left to the process of nature. I have great confusion of mind over this Bill, because, like other Senators, I have been so absorbed in the very exciting matters which came before the Seanad in the last few days that I confess this finds some of us in a very ignorant condition, which may compel some Senators to vote against the Bill who, with greater knowledge, might vote for it. I would like that the Minister would give us all information possible on this Bill. [VI, 259-60]

42. DESIGN OF COINAGE

March 3, 1926. Coinage Bill, 1926: Second Stage.

MR. YEATS: I wish to take this opportunity to thank the Minister for Finance for the speech which he made in the Dáil promising to get together a competent, artistic committee to advise on the designs of our coinage. The official designs of the Government, especially its designs in connection with postage stamps and coinage, may be described, I think, as the silent ambassadors of national taste. The Government had now taken the right step. They may not get a beautiful coinage; it is difficult to get beauty of any kind. At any rate, the Government has the right ambition. Two days ago I had a letter from an exceedingly famous decorative artist, in which he described the postage stamps of this country as at once the humblest and ugliest in the world. At any rate, our coinage design will, I hope, be such that even the humblest citizen will be proud of it.* [VI, 502]

* Yeats's hopes for a beautiful coinage were not, in fact, disappointed. An unusually intelligent and vigorous committee was appointed by the government, with Yeats as its Chairman. The Committee set to work in June, 1926, and seventeen meetings later, in

43. CONDITION OF SCHOOLS

March 24, 1926. School Attendance Bill, 1925: Second Stage.

DR. YEATS: I had hoped that Senator Brown would be here and that it would not have fallen on me to speak on this measure. Since this Bill passed through the Dáil much new evidence has come to our hands, which, I think, we should take into consideration. I have been reading the reports of the various inspectors. I think I will have the feeling of the Seanad with me when I say that we should not force the children into schools unless we have such assurance from the Government as will make us satisfied that these schools will be put into a fit condition to receive the children. I will read here the words of one of the inspectors: "There is a very considerable number of school buildings ill-adapted in the first case to serve as schools, and now in a bad state of repair, damp, uncomfortable, and often insanitary. A few are mere hovels, yet frequently overcrowded, a menace to the health of the children and teachers, an eyesore to the passers-by and a standing reflection on all responsible for their condition." That is an extract from the report by Mr. Tierney. He has reported on the general condition of the schools in his area. He is inspector for Mayo, part of Leinster, the whole of County Longford, and portions of Westmeath. You have practically in every inspector's report something of the same

---

April, 1928, had completed its task, after following a procedure which the Master of the Royal Mint in London took occasion to refer to as a scheme so admirable "that it might serve as a model for any Government embarking on the difficult task of obtaining designs for a new coinage." Yeats's buoyant and delightful epistle "What We Did or Tried to Do," which opens the Government report (*Coinage of Saorstat Eireann*, 1928), is included in Appendix III.

kind. A majority of the schools are not in this condition but evidently a very considerable minority of the schools are in this condition.

Speaking on this matter on the 11th of June last the President said:

Before I leave this question of primary education, I should mention that there is one further matter—also an important matter in our quest for efficiency—with which the Minister for Education hopes to deal as soon as possible. This country has always suffered from the inadequacy of its school buildings. The disturbances of recent years have left us still more seriously in arrears in this important particular, and the operation of an effective School Attendance Act will increase still more the lack of proper accommodation for primary education. To meet this difficulty the Department of Education is having a thorough census made of the primary-school-buildings of the Saorstat, and when this is complete, it may be necessary to ask you to make further provision in the Estimates to bring the primary school accommodation up to the level necessary for complete efficiency.

Now we have not had those further statistics as to the state of the schools. We do not know whether the Government will be able, whether it will get that necessary support to put all these schools right. But it should be our business to see that it gets that support. I should like also to suggest to the Seanad that the proper method of doing this is not under the Estimates. I hold that this should be done by a national loan. It is a non-recurrent expenditure, precisely the kind of expenditure that is usually met by a loan. One feels that if the vote is put on the Estimates that it will not be adequately and amply dealt with. I would like to do something further. I suggest to the Government that they should appoint a commission to consider the whole question of school buildings in the State. A great effort should be made to put these schools right, and that means that the attention of the country should be drawn to the matter. Furthermore, we should see that the right methods are taken and that the right form of school buildings is adopted. The Government has already a commission inquiring into the school curriculum, but they have not a commission set up for the purpose of inquiring into the school buildings. My suggestion is that it should be a point of honour to the Seanad not to ask the school children to enter those buildings until they are certain that those buildings are fit to receive the children.

To be able to do my duty as a Senator in relation to this question, I, myself, before this Government report was put into my hands, saw a number of the schools. I saw schools in Dublin and in the country. I was shocked by what I saw in the Dublin schools. I saw schools where the children were learning their lessons by artificial light at noon-day, because the windows were too small. I saw schools where two classes were being held side by side, because there was not room to give a separate class to each. That means wear and tear to the nerves of the children and to the temper of the teachers.

I also saw another thing to which I wish to draw the attention of the Government. Many of these schools are filthy. A minority of the children who come to them, I should say a substantial minority, are filthy. There are no adequate basins, sometimes no basins at all, in which the children could wash themselves. I have seen schools where the children are perfectly clean. I have seen one school in Dublin where the floors are washed once a week and brushed every day. Many of the country schools are never washed at all. I have seen a school lately in a South of Ireland town managed by the Sisters of Mercy, and it is a model to all schools. There the part of the house that is used frequently is washed once a week and brushed daily. The children are perfectly clean. What can be done there can be done elsewhere in Ireland. But you cannot have these things done unless the country is prepared to spend the money.

It should be a matter of honour to the State no matter how poor it may be, to spend that money. You must not, for instance, do what is almost always done—get this work done by the children. It must not be the business of the children to keep the school clean after they have done their day's work in the school. There must be properly appointed people to see that the school is clean and also to see that the children are clean and that they are sent to school clean. When the children are not clean, they should be made wash themselves in a proper place provided in the school. If you do not do that you will not have a centre of civilization in the schools and the children might as well remain at home. I think you cannot secure any of these things without more expense, and, of course, a more efficient system of inspection, than you have at present. The inspectors who come from the central authority will not be able to keep an eye on all these things. There is an obvious way out of the difficulty, a way which we cannot take, perhaps, but a way which the North of Ireland has taken, and that is to put the care of the school buildings in the hands of local committees.

One of the Government inspectors strongly urges that upon the Government. That is done practically all over Europe. It is done in Catholic Austria as it is done in Protestant Scandinavia. The committees differ from country to country. They are constituted in various ways, but I think these committees exist practically everywhere. I should like to add that the difficulty in appointing those committees does not come from one religion alone. It comes just as much, if I understand it, from the religion in which I was born as it comes from any other, but it is not to the credit of the State that no way can be found out of the difficulty. If we cannot have local inspection, which would mean inspection by inspectors who have local knowledge, then we must devise some equally efficient method.

There is one thing on which I feel strongly. As long as you carry on the present obsolete method of education in your schools you will have the usual strain between the master and the pupil. You will have the usual problem of children being punished by a master with a bad temper, and your only way to prevent that is when the so-called punishment books are regularly kept. Those are books in which the teacher is bound to record the punishment inflicted, and why it is inflicted. My experience is that those punishment books are not kept because there is not sufficiently adequate inspection. I do not say that the present inspectors are not most able men, but you want more numerous inspection or better local inspection to secure efficiency in those things. If the Government can convince me that it is able and willing to make these buildings suitable for the children, that is to say, to make them clean and sanitary—and many of them are not sanitary—to make the floor space sufficient and to make them reasonably cheerful, I am prepared to give my unimportant vote in favour of this Bill. If they do not, I cannot give it.

I am not asking anything extravagant. I think we ought to do whatever is done by other countries of the same wealth as this nation in order to ensure the welfare of our children. We should consider, for instance, that there are at present some arrangements, not I think always very wise, as to the feeding of school-children in the towns. There are none in the country, and judging by my own countryside, where I live during the summer months, it is needed. Children will start early in the morning. They will be the greater portion of the day in school and they will have no adequate meals. They come away hungry, and it seems, if not very necessary, at least very desirable that they should have food. Then, of course, many other countries, perhaps not richer than this, have found means of seeing that children are properly clothed and that they have proper books. These are all difficult but desirable things.

I have no desire to speak on the question of the curriculum. It is being considered by a Commission at this moment. I wish that the Government had introduced a comprehensive educational measure dealing with all the details before asking us to compel children, by law, to go into the schools. Whether it is good for the children or not depends not only on the building but on the nature of the system under which they are taught. I am sure for a child to spend all day in school with a stupid, ill-trained man under an ill-planned system, is less good for that child than that the child should be running through the fields and learning nothing. I should like to draw the attention of the Government to one nation which has reformed its educational system in the most suggestive and profound way; that is Italy. It has not produced a system unique to Italy. It has simply gathered together the results of experiments all over the world. They are now teaching a system of education adapted to an agricultural nation like this or Italy, a system of education that will not turn out clerks only, but will turn out efficient men and women who can manage to do all the work of the nation. This system has been tried in Ireland. There are some schools carrying it out. There is one large primary school managed by nuns in the South of Ireland which has adopted practically the entire Italian system and which is carrying it out with great effect, and has found that it is applicable, and that its teachers do not need special training to carry it out. The Italian Minister who adopted that policy was warned by everyone that it would not be possible to get this elaborate system carried out by partly educated people. It has been proved possible and of great benefit to the children.

In order to give an intelligent vote—at one time I thought it would be a silent one—on this question I have kept two clear principles in my mind. One is that we ought to be able to give the child of the poor as good an education as we give to the child of the rich. Of course the rich man's child remains longer at school. I have consulted teachers and people accustomed to the latest methods of education, and they are all clear that there is no reason why the education of the children of the poor should not be as good, while it lasts, as the education of the children of the rich. I would like to suggest another principle, that the child itself must be the end in education. It is a curious thing how many times the education of Europe has drifted into error. For two or three centuries people thought that their various religious systems were more important than the child. In the modern world the tendency is to think of the nation; that it is more important than the child. In Japan, I understand, the child is sacrificed to patriotism. I have seen education unified in America, so that the child is sacrificed to that of unified Americanism, and the human mind is codified. We are bound to go

through the same passion ourselves. There is a tendency to subordinate the child to the idea of the nation. I suggest that whether we teach either Irish history, Anglo-Irish literature or Gaelic, we should always see that the child is the object and not any of our special purposes.*
[VI, 519-25]

44. CONDITION OF SCHOOLS

March 30, 1926. Central Fund Bill, 1926.

DR. YEATS: I remember when I was a boy meeting an elderly man going to vote for the County Council in Acton, and I said to him: "You know nothing about County Council affairs, really?" "No," he said, "I know nothing whatever; I do not know one man there more than another, but there is one man who is going to spend money and I am going to vote for him." I said, "Why," and he said, "Because he has everyone against him," and he added a little later, "He must be a man of conviction."

Now I rise to ask for more consideration for those men of conviction who think that the vote on the estimates for Irish education is completely inadequate. I am not sure that I should have raised the question except for the very surprising speech made by Senator Sir John Keane in the last debate, when he said that whatever was spent upon making the Irish schools sanitary for the children should be taken by economies out of the present votes for Irish schools. We have all great respect for Senator Sir John Keane as a financial expert. I can only suppose he made that statement because he had never given any attention whatever to the question. I have gone to quite obvious sources

* A speech on Irish Education which Yeats gave three months earlier to the "Irish Literary Society," and printed in George Russell's *The Irish Statesman,* spells out his views on education in interesting ways. (See Appendix IV.)

to get the latest information. I have gone to the Encyclopedia Britannica and one or two other obvious sources, and I want to draw attention to the fact that in Ireland we spend on education only £1 6s. od. per head of the population; in Scotland they spend about £2 10s. od. per head of the population. That is to say, they spend £11,000,000 as against our four-and-a-half millions, having a population about one-third greater than ours. In England they spend about £2 10s. per head of the population on education. In the North of Ireland they lately increased their parliamentary grant for education, while they have also added to it by rates, and therefore they are spending more on education than we are. It is impossible, at the moment, to find the exact figure. Let us turn now to other small countries which we are accustomed to compare with ourselves and see how they deal with education. Denmark is spending about £2 15s. od. per head on education. Norway is spending about the same, £2 15s. od. per head on education. I do not know what endowments, apart from parliamentary expenditure, Denmark and Norway have, but I think I can safely say that England and Scotland have far greater endowments for education than this country and that there is a further increase from this source in the amount of money spent on education in England and Scotland.

President Cosgrave said on the 11th June last year he was quite aware of the fact that there would have to be an increased grant for Irish education. I am not therefore in any way criticizing the Government. I am sure that they know these figures and are anxious adequately to finance Irish education, but I think it is important this House should know these figures. I do not think the President's proposed method of dealing with the question is the most desirable. He spoke of an increase in the Estimates. I think that will lead, especially at this time of depression, to the sum voted being entirely inadequate to make the schools even tolerably sanitary, and I think the right method is through a national loan. The whole sum ought not to fall upon this generation. The repayment of it should be distributed over several generations; but when you have put the schools right you require money to keep them right. Inspectors of schools have pointed out in reports that managers have no funds to keep the schools clean and in repair and some other method will have to be found obviously.

I see by the "Irish Times" this morning that the Executive of the Irish National Teachers' Association has put down a resolution for its coming conference in favour of local committees, and of a rate to keep the schools in repair, and to keep them in a sanitary condition. The "Irish Times" article draws special attention to the fact that these bodies will be representative of the parents and that it is essential to have representatives of the parents if the schools are to be kept in a condition approximating in comfort and health to the homes in which the children live. The "Irish Times" article was very vigorous and very thoughtful, and I should think it should help to remove a good deal of the opposition to the local committees that is exhibited at present by certain managers belonging to the Church of Ireland. I think the Teachers' Association will have to use their utmost vigour to rouse public opinion if the Government is to do what they consider right in this matter. It will be said: Can we afford to make the schools sanitary considering how poor we are? I can only use the words of the Australian Minister for Education when questioned in the same way; he said: "It is precisely because we are poor that we must spend money on our schools."

I doubt if any nation can become prosperous unless it has national faith, and one very important part of national faith is faith in its resources, faith both in the richness of its soil and the richness of its intellect, and I am convinced that as much wealth can come from the intellect of Ireland as will come from the soil and that the one will repay cultivation as much as the other. [VI, 645-47]

45. CONDITION OF SCHOOLS

April 28, 1926. School Attendance Bill.

DR. YEATS: I should like to draw the attention of the Seanad to Article I of the Convention of Geneva which, I understand, was signed by the representative of the Irish Free State:

"Children under the age of fourteen years may not be employed or worked in any public or private agricultural undertaking, or any branch thereof, save outside the hours fixed for school attendance. If they are employed outside the hours of school attendance the employment shall not be such as to prejudice their attendance at school."

That article certainly represents the opinion of the great majority of those identified with the teaching of children all over the world, and I do not think the Free State should depart from it. It is very doubtful if it is keeping within the spirit of it, as it is, in view of the exemptions that are given at certain seasons of the year, but I am quite certain the Seanad will not support any resolution which makes further breaches in the Convention of Geneva. I would like to point out to the Seanad again that we are spending on the education of our children what amounts to £1 5s. per head of the population per annum. In England and Scotland they spend about £2 10s. per head of the population per annum. Our trade rival, Denmark, spends what amounts to about £2 15s. per head of the population. In Norway the proportion is about the same. Of course that is counting not only taxes but rates, and shows that already our education is starved. It is certain that our children are going into the battle of life very poorly equipped to face rivals, to put it no higher. In any case the children are going into the battle of life unequipped because enough is not spent on education. The proposal in the amendment is that the inefficient education the children are being given should be made still more inefficient.* [VII, 6-7]

Amendment put and negatived.

46. SENATE MEMBERSHIP

June 15, 1926. Message from the Dáil. President Cosgrave in attendance. The resolution would have made ineligible for membership in the Dáil or the Senate certain State employees, such as teachers, since they would be unable to attend to their duties properly if they attended the meetings of the Dáil or Senate.

AN CATHAOIRLEACH: The following Message has been received from the Dáil:

Dáil Eireann has passed the following Resolution, in which the concurrence of Seanad Eireann is desired:

"That it is expedient that a Joint Committee of both Houses of the Oireachtas consisting of three members of the Dáil and three members of the Seanad, with power to send for persons, papers and records, be set up to inquire and report whether the incapacity to be elected to, or to sit as a member of, either House of the Oireachtas imposed as regards certain classes of persons by Sections 51 and 57 of the Electoral Act, 1923 (No. 12 of 1923) should be extended to include any other class or classes of persons, and, if so, to what class or classes should the incapacity extend."

MR. YEATS: We have all great respect for President Cosgrave. He is not a member of this House but he comes to us and asks us to appoint a Committee which would possibly disqualify certain members of this House from the right to be elected to sit in the Seanad. I

---

* Sec. 4 of the amendment included a clause which provided that until 1936 a child 12 years old or over might be absent from school from the 17th of March to the 15th of May, and from August 1 to October 15, by reason of being engaged "in light agricultural work for his parent on his parent's land."

feel we owe it to the honour and dignity of this House not to permit any kind of committee or tribunal calling in question their right to be elected and sit here, unless a very strong case indeed can be made for it. We had a resolution brought forward at first without the intention of making any case for it whatever. We have to use a great effort to get any sort of statement of facts whatever. I do not think any member of this House understood the first statement made by the President.

It is most necessary that we should have the assistance in our Legislature of the best technical types. In the near future, we shall have to consider many things in connection with education and it is most necessary that the opinions of the teachers should be represented in both Houses. In the recent debates in the Dáil one man whose knowledge and opinion were of the utmost value to the Dáil was a teacher—Deputy O'Connell. No member of either House, as far I can make out by a careful study of his and other speeches, possesses knowledge comparable to his on the whole question of education in this country. I do not think that his position will be affected by this Committee, but where a man of such technical knowledge has been found once he can be found again. We require to have that technical knowledge in this House for the next two or three years. I hope I am a benevolent man, and I think I am an unsuspicious man, but I find it difficult to separate this resolution from some preceding events.

Some months ago an organisation of teachers passed a resolution in favour of local control of school buildings, that is to say, that these buildings should be controlled and kept in order by local committees.

Very considerable opposition arose to that object from the managers, and it is only right I should say not from the managers of one denomination only but a very considerable opposition came also from the Protestant managers, who did not like Protestant schools passing under the control of Catholic committees.

It is not a sectarian question. It is a question of the ecclesiastical mind, Protestant and Catholic on the one side, and on the other a very great deal of the most intelligent lay opinion in Ireland. Then two or three weeks ago the Catholic Managerial Association passed a resolution in favour of repairs to schools and claiming that the money for the repairs should be given to the managers for that purpose, and they added to the resolution a rider that the schools in Ireland are in a fairly good condition, which they are not. They know the arrangements for the maintenance of schools have broken down, and it was admitted that the schools are now in a bad condition. I read in the papers that "Certain pressure was brought upon the President." I think that is the diplomatic and journalistic way of putting it, and then we have this resolution. As I have said, the President, a man for whom we have the utmost respect, has come and asked us to appoint a tribunal to consider the eligibility of certain of our members. I suggest that behind the President there is a certain pressure asking him to have a tribunal appointed. I think a much stronger case must be made before this House votes for the establishment of any such tribunal. [VII, 415-17]

President's motion carried.

47. THE LANE PICTURES

July 14, 1926. On a motion requesting the Government to pass a resolution designed to bring the Lane pictures back to Ireland.

DR. YEATS: It will be within the memory of Senators that some two years ago both this House and the Dáil passed resolutions urging the British Government to give effect to the unwitnessed codicil of Sir Hugh Lane's will. Lord Glenavy gave his very emphatic opinion at the time that it was impossible to doubt that Sir Hugh Lane did intend that codicil as his last will and testament. The only satisfactory thing in the report issued some two weeks ago by the British Government is that it also decides that Sir Hugh Lane did intend that codicil for his last will and testament. Senator Brown and others have analysed and exposed the excuses made by the Commission and accepted by the British Government for not giving effect to that decision. In this country we have to decide upon a course of action, and it is largely with that object that I speak. It has been a long dispute; some of us have given much time and thought to it; my closest friend, Lady Gregory, has given the best of her thought and much of her time to it for the last ten years. The property involved, though great in monetary value, is more than property, for it means the possession of the implements of national culture. You will forgive me if I forget that I am occasionally a politician, and remember that I am always a man of letters and speak less diplomatically and with less respect for institutions and great names than is, perhaps, usual in public life. In our endeavour to have our case laid before the British public once more, to have the fallacies of this report exposed, we are faced with an unexpected difficulty. Three weeks ago, while the report was still unissued, when the British Government had announced no decision, when the whole matter was *sub-judice* between the nations, the King opened the new wing of the Tate Gallery, that is to say, the building which, it is claimed, was built to contain these pictures by Sir Joseph Duveen, and of which they are the principal ornament. As he made his speech, or as he passed through the gallery to deliver it, his eyes must constantly have looked upon the words, "Lane Bequest."

It is the policy of most of us in this country, seeing that very lately we preferred a king to a president and that we fought a civil war that we might be governed by a king rather than a president, to remain upon the friendliest terms with the King of England, who is also the King of Ireland. We have been told I do not know whether truthfully or not, that the King is personally friendly to us, that a certain speech which influenced our affairs for good was made on his own initiative. Statements of that kind are frequently untrue; they are put out for policy, but, whether true or not, we have no desire to disturb the impression that they have left. Our relations with Ulster make this more essential. But it would be impossible to preserve this attitude towards Royalty if certain obvious conditions are ignored. When the King was urged to perform an action which seriously compromised the claim made by this nation, when he was urged to intervene in this international dispute, was it pointed out to him that he should be advised not only by his English Ministers alone, but also by the Governor-General, or otherwise by his Irish Ministers? We have no means of questioning Ministers in this House, and I would be glad, therefore, if someone in the Dáil would ask President Cosgrave if his Government was consulted before the King recently opened the new modern gallery in London. Important as our claim for the Lane pictures is, this question seems to me to raise an issue of far greater importance, one vitally affecting the constitutional position not only of this country but of every Dominion. I can imagine the British Government replying in the evasive spirit of its Commission that as our claim was moral and not legal the King was not bound to take cognizance of it, but in disputes between nations—and the British Government itself has, within its terms of reference to the Commission, called this dispute international—it is not legal but moral and material issues that cause trouble. A day may come when the action of the King may prejudice some claim involving the most fundamental rights. I see by the daily papers that Canada and the Irish Free State are to seek at the next Imperial Conference for some clarification or modification of the relations between the Crown and the Dominions. I think that this recent experience of ours shows that one or the other is necessary.

When I addressed this House some two years ago on this question I believed that our case was almost won, and from that day to about three weeks before the issue of the report we had continual assurances that it had been practically decided in our favour. The persons who gave us these assurances seemed to be in a position to know. I am certain of their sincerity. If you ask me about the sincerity of those from whom they derived their information, I can merely say that I am without conviction, one way or the other. What happened at the last moment is unknown to me. I am sure of one thing; it was not any particular force or authority in the report of the Commission that made the change. Senator Brown has dealt effectively with the two or three reasons which they give for retaining in London property which they admit that Sir Hugh Lane intended for Dublin, and believe that he had legally bequeathed to Dublin. Of these arguments, that which seems to have weighed most with English public opinion, and probably with the Commission, is the statement put forward by the Tate Gallery and accepted by the Commission, that Sir Joseph Duveen received a promise on June 9th, 1916, that if he were to build a new wing to the Tate Gallery Sir Hugh Lane's pictures should be deposited there. I hold letters in my hand which will prove conclusively that no such promise was ever given. These letters were not laid before the Commission, because it never passed through the minds of the three witnesses, Lady Gregory, Mrs. Shine and myself, that the Commission would go outside its reference, nor did it occur to the Commissioners to question us upon this point. They had been appointed to find out whether Sir Hugh Lane intended the codicil to be a legal document, and whether, if so, considering the international issue involved, it should be given effect to. It never occurred to us that they would repudiate their reference, and declare that there was no international issue involved, and then go into a mass of detail which seemed excluded by that reference. Before repudiating their reference they should have referred the matter back to the English Government for a new reference, and have informed us of their action. If such a promise had been given, it would have carried no weight, for it would have been given by one party in the dispute without the knowledge of the other, but it was not given, as I shall now show.

Sir Hugh Lane was drowned in the "Lusitania" on May 7th, 1915, and at the end of that month Lady Gregory laid the codicil before the Chairman of the Board of Governors of the English National Gallery, which had the custody of the pictures. I have here a letter written by her on June 6th of that year to a great New York connoisseur and collector:

I went to see (taking a copy of the codicil) Lord Curzon, the most active of the London National Gallery trustees, and one who appreciates most of the French pictures. He would, of course, like to keep them but said he thought Hugh's wishes, so clearly expressed, ought to be respected, and he would say that when the time comes to the other trustees.

On June 1st, 1915, that is to say, three or four days before the date of the letter I have just quoted, Lady Gregory received the following letter from Lord Curzon:

I mentioned to-day to the National Gallery Board the subject which you had been good enough to bring before me the evening before. . . . I think the right thing would be for the executors to address them formally through solicitors, and lay the whole case before them.

On September 15th Lord Curzon wrote as follows:

It seems to be a matter in which the executors will have to formally approach the Board, who will, no doubt, consult their solicitors.

A year later I was in London and heard privately that the National Gallery intended to have a gallery built for modern French pictures, and to put the Lane collection into it. I told Lady Gregory of this, and she wrote to Lord Curzon, who answered as follows on October 10th, 1916:

The matter is not in my hands nor at this moment even in the hands of the Board. They are waiting to be advised by their legal advisers, and in the interim it would not be right for any individual trustee to intervene.

Yet our opponents allege, and the Commission accepts their allegation, that an individual trustee did intervene. Here are the words of the report:

Not only has the London Gallery the legal possession of the pictures but, on the assurance that such a gift would be in perpetuity, it has secured the gift of a gallery in which the pictures are to be housed.

An editorial in the Burlington Magazine for 1924 gives the precise date and circumstance of the alleged promise:

On June 9th, 1916, Sir Joseph Duveen, being on the point of returning to America, saw Lord D'Abernon about the project.

It then goes on to say that Lord D'Abernon thereupon promised the pictures if Sir Joseph Duveen built the gallery.

I have read you the assurances of the Chairman of the Board, Lord Curzon, stating that the matter was undecided, assurances repeated several times for more than a year, the last and most specific, that in which he states that no individual governor had the right to intervene, being written some months after the date of the alleged promise. Relying upon those repeated assurances we had summoned no meetings, organised neither petitions nor protest, and we were right. It was entirely impossible that a man of Lord Curzon's position and training would have deliberately deceived us. Unless minutes of the National Gallery recording that promise were laid before the Commission, I have a right to affirm that such a promise was never given. Sir Joseph Duveen or Mr. McCall imagined the whole thing, or Lord D'Abernon made some vague statement which was misinterpreted. The matter is very serious, a very large amount of property is involved, property which may already be worth some £200,000 and which will certainly rise in value from year to year. I, therefore, ask the Irish Government to press upon the British Government the production of the minutes of the Board of Governors of the National Gallery of London for the period during which the promise is stated to have been made. If no such minute can be discovered then the Commission has been grossly misled; if it is discovered, we have.

I was going to deal with the other indefinite argument, that if Sir Hugh Lane had lived he would have changed his mind. He was the most generous of men. A famous artist said of him that he had raised the profession of a picture dealer into the magnificence of the Medici. Had he lived I have no doubt he would have given great endowments right and left to Dublin, to London, and to that great gallery in South Africa that was partly his foundation. But when he was going on that last voyage he knew he had only one collection of pictures to bequeath.

He preferred to bequeath them, where the rest of his bequests had gone, to the gallery which will always bear his name, where everything had been chosen by himself, and where they were not to be lost among the growing richness of the great London gallery.

There is that other argument—I am not competent to deal with it—that there is no precedent for altering a will. While we do not press that point I have heard great lawyers differ on it. The other day the "Independent" newspaper—and I should like to thank the "Independent" newspaper for the great vigour with which it is pressing this question—gave a very remarkable precedent. In the midst of the Great War, by Act of Parliament, the will of Cecil Rhodes was modified. In that case there was no question of the letter of the will or of his intentions. He had left a large bequest to enable German students to attend certain English universities. They abrogated that request not merely for the time of the war but for ever. That is precisely one of those actions which all nations do in time of war and are ashamed of afterwards. Yet it seems to me if we had claimed that we would not make an excessive claim. It seems to me what they did by Act of Parliament to modify the will of Cecil Rhodes under the influence of national hatred they might well be asked to do—to modify the will of Sir Hugh Lane under the influence of national honour. Now what are we to do? No compromise. We ask and we must continue to ask our right—to hold 39 pictures, and for ever. Let the Dublin Commissioners build that long-promised gallery. We have already, in Harcourt Street, great treasures that will make it one of the richest galleries in the world. Let them build that gallery and let them see there is ample space for these 39 pictures. Let them write the names of the pictures on the wall, in spaces reserved for them, and let the codicil be displayed in some conspicuous place and watch the public opinion of these countries. I do not believe that the public opinion of these countries will permit the London Gallery to retain pictures which it was not the intention of the donor to leave to it. [VII, 1017-23]

Motion carried.

48. JUDGES' COSTUMES

July 22, 1926. High Court and Supreme Court Rules.

DR. YEATS: I move:—

To insert before the word "received" the word "not" and to add at the end of the motion the words "with the exception of Order 30, Rules 2 and 3."

This amendment is to delete that portion of the rules which prescribes the present robes and wigs of the Judges of the High Court and the Supreme Court. I move this, not because I desire to see the judges sitting in their courts in ordinary costume, but because I believe that the Government have in their possession very much finer designs than any that has come down to us. I am sorry that the Government have not found some means of making these designs known to this House, because the House has to vote on the subject. They might have been laid on the Table of the House. You are asked to vote in favour of designs without knowing what the alternative to these designs is. The only guidance that this House might perhaps possess is that new designs have been adopted for the District Court, and photographs of these designs have appeared in the papers.

AN CATHAOIRLEACH: That is not quite accurate. We had better be accurate about this. That has to be done by Rules of Court and I notice that the District Court Rules omit any reference to it. They cannot adopt any costume they like, but only in accordance with the rules of Court. They have not framed any Rules of Court for such a purpose.

DR. YEATS: They have not adopted any costumes, but we have seen the costumes that have been reproduced. They are certainly very dignified and very simple. They are, I think, more dignified and more simple than any costumes worn in any magistrates' courts in these islands. The robes were designed by a celebrated Irish artist, Sir Charles Shannon, and the cap was designed at the Dun Emer Works, and admirably designed. However, in the circumstances I cannot ask you to vote in favour of other designs, because I cannot put the designs before you. But I suggest if you reject the present robes and wigs, the Government will have to lay before you new designs by somebody, and then we will know whether or not we will have a better type. When you think over the present costume, that great grey wig and that gown, if you try to see it without historical associations, is it not something incredibly fantastic? Is it not something essentially preposterous? Of course, I admit that historical associations and tradition can endear anything; I will admit that the judge's wig is endeared to me by historic associations and tradition. Historical traditions have endeared the small foot of the Chinese woman, have endeared the nose-ring. I admit that I find it very difficult to realise how preposterous the judge's wig is. I am in the position of some man in China who finds it impossible to realise the preposterousness of the small foot, but it is so. Historical associations are great things. I do not think we should lightly put them aside, even when we endear something which is, in itself, without dignity or honour. Historical associations give honour and they give dignity.

But this country has passed through one of those crises which all countries have made the occasion of a new act of energy for the creation of tradition. No country that I know, after a revolution such as we have gone through, has been content to take without examination the traditions of the past, and I cannot imagine any place where innovation is more necessary than in the outward image of the law. One of the greatest arguments with which we have been familiar for generations in favour of the self-government of this country, was that the law as practised here was regarded by great numbers of people as something inherently alien. We all want the people to realise that the law is now their own creation, their own instrument, and any external change which marks that fact will in some degree—I will not say in a great degree—help the people to understand that the judges are their own judges and not judges imposed upon them from without. I speak especially of the judges. I think the case of the barristers is somewhat different. They are not paid out of public money. They are a free corporation. I should be prepared to leave the barristers to time and to public opinion. But the Government cannot put aside responsibility for the judges, because the judges are paid with Government money, and—always provided, remember, that they possess better designs, designs inherently of greater dignity and of greater nobility than those in present use—I can see every reason for the adoption of these designs, and I can see no sufficient case against the adoption. The designs for the Supreme Court and for the High Court which the Government possess are, in my belief, designs of great dignity, great beauty and simplicity. They would do honour to any country, and in adopting them this country would do as well as the Vatican did when it permitted Michael Angelo to set aside one does not know what historical traditions, and to design the costumes of the Papal Guards.

SIR JOHN KEANE: I am afraid I shall not be able to deal with this matter with the same scholarship and in the same eloquent language as that used by Senator Yeats, but as a plain man, I should like to make certain observations upon this proposal. I think we should be very cautious, and should have very good reasons before we break with tradition.

MRS. COSTELLO: English tradition?

SIR JOHN KEANE: Yes, English tradition. I am not ashamed to say English tradition. It is the tradition which the people have grown accustomed to. . . . I do not see why we should do violence to tradition in respect to the costume of our judges. The Senator referred to the present head-dress of our judges as preposterous, but I can conceive great practical value in that head-dress. I was looking up literary references as to what I believe is the proposed new head-dress known as the biretta. I have not much knowledge of the biretta, but I find a reference to it in the Athenaeum in these words: "a person described as with a black shock of hair emerging or appearing under his red biretta." I can conceive nothing more inartistic than that, because hair may not be always black, it may be sometimes grey or brown, it may be long or short, or a person may have no hair. Moreover, we may now have ladies joining the legal profession. I see nothing in the ordinary course of development to prevent ladies rising to seats upon the Bench. Ladies have a great variety of head-dress which would also contrast in a very incongruous manner with such a close-fitting ornament as the biretta.

The wig has the virtue of uniformity and covers up all these imperfections of the flesh and gives very dignified results. You get uniformity. That is for what it is worth. When we go further into the matter I confess I was interested in the quarter from which this proposal came. My memory at once went back to a recent speech delivered by Senator Yeats in this House on the subject of the Lane pictures, when he used these words. "You will forgive me if I forget that I am occasionally a politician and remember that I am always a man of letters, and speak less diplomatically and with less respect for institutions and great names than is, perhaps, usual in public life." Following up that trend of thought I remember certain verses of the Senator's in which his words seem to me rather inconsistent with the remarks that I have just quoted. He writes:

> "All things can tempt me from this craft of verse;
> One time it was a woman's face, or worse—
> The seeming needs of my fool-driven land."*

DR. GOGARTY: What is the date?

SIR JOHN KEANE: I do not know.

DR. GOGARTY: It is all-important.

SIR JOHN KEANE: . . . If I am told I am wrong I shall not pursue the argument any further, but I am told—that the new head-dress is to be the biretta. That will bring close together the outward association between the Church and the Judiciary which had been widening steadily

* In *The Green Helmet and Other Poems*, 1910.

down the ages. We find full justification in verses written by the Senator himself:

> "How but in custom and in ceremony
> Are innocence and beauty born?
> Ceremony's a name for the rich horn
> And Custom for the spreading laurel tree."*

If I understand that rightly, the rich horn is that of plenty which we all desire, and the laurel tree is that of fame to which we aspire.

DR. GOGARTY: . . . The important things in the country are often the little things, like the flag, for instance, which are of the utmost importance—more important than words can express, because they are the spiritual and symbolic things. The costume of our lawgivers is one of those little important, significant things. It is important to us because by it we are to judge whether the old regime of law, which meant misery and oppression to this country for many centuries, is at an end or is not at an end. We want to see a change of heart accompanied by a change of costume. Who can tell the thousands of our fellow-countrymen who faced the wig and gown before being condemned to death, transportation, or penal servitude, for political offences in the old evil days? One would expect from a learned and great profession, to say the least of it, a little good taste in this matter and not a wish to perpetuate the association of the wig and gown, inevitable in the Irish mind, with injustice and place-hunting. The ingratiating barrister, the transporting judge—all were clothed in this ridiculous remnant of the 18th century. Senator Sir John Keane says the alternative is a biretta. There is no such thing. I have seen the drawing. The cap at present might be called a biretta if it were flattened out, starched and stiffened. It is a flat velvet cap which, without disguising a judge lends to him dignity and a little amount of beauty, things hitherto not associated in this country with the law. We are told to respect custom. But is custom to date only from the advent of the English into this country.

---

* "A Prayer for My Daughter," 1921.

There were customs and traditions in this country which preceded English law by about a thousand years. There were both humanity and equity. The Brehon Laws were more humane than the English laws and more equitable and humane than the Roman. In the treatment of prisoners they were equal to the most modern form of treatment as seen in Italy. There was no such thing as capital punishment under the Brehon Laws. They exceeded Italian laws in their commonsense. They made a malefactor work to compensate those who suffered.

.   .   .   .

EARL OF MAYO: . . . Senator Yeats talked about historical associations, about honour and about dignity. He also talked about the small foot of the Chinese woman. I know something about that, as a nephew of mine who is a naval officer spent two years in that country. He told me that the small Chinese foot was invented by the mandarins, who did not wish their ladies to leave the precincts of their houses. These ladies were kept in these houses in many cases against their will. That is the explanation of the small foot of the Chinese woman, so that I do not think it is a very happy historical association.

. . . Senator Gogarty said that a change of heart should be followed by a change of costume. I cannot follow that. I do not see how a person could change his heart by putting on a poplin robe or any other robe. All those who follow the profession of the law respect the judges, as they gain their positions by hard work, integrity and honour. Those who dwell in the British Isles in these civilised days and who did not live when the Brehons ruled have, by long custom, respected the judges with their wigs on their heads. A wig is a most becoming costume for the head, especially for a bald head. If a man has an intelligent and a fairly good-looking face, as can be seen in many pictures, the wig makes him appear a very good-looking man. All artists admit that. It is a becoming and a dignified headgear. This is not a question of policy. Surely those who follow the law might be allowed to wear on their heads the dress they like. Imagine being tried by a judge with a black velvet cap. I should at once associate myself, if I was on trial, with a criminal in the dock who was going to get the longest possible sentence. The feelings and the emotions of a judge who is wearing a wig are not disclosed. I think the first time that an innocent person appeared before a judge wearing a black cap he would say to himself, "This is the end of me. I may as well say my prayers at once." I shall certainly vote against Senator Yeats's amendment.

MR. KENNY: . . . I would like to correct a possible impression made by the remarks of Senator the Earl of Mayo in regard to the small foot of the Chinese woman. In China that is a characteristic of the nobility; a small foot is a symbol of nobility amongst Chinese women just the same as a long finger-nail on the left hand is a symbol of nobility on the part of a Chinese man. I have seen a Chinaman's finger-nail so long as to take the form of a corkscrew. How they preserve their nails in that fashion I do not know. I have seen a Chinese mandarin with finger-nails three and four inches in length. They are very particular about preserving that very unsightly mark of their nobility. The whole thing simply means that the Chinese woman with the small foot is differentiated from and segregated from the labouring classes. Similarly with the mandarin whose finger-nails are allowed to grow. It goes without saying that the woman with the clubbed foot and the man who has devoted the whole of his life to preserving his finger-nails cannot have done much labouring work.

·   ·   ·   ·

DR. YEATS: If we assume for a moment that this is a desirable thing, that it is possible to put the judges into costumes that are appropriate to the country, do you think that a very old man, grown old in the use of quite a different costume, would ever accept the change? Never. Impossible. If the change is desirable—there is no way out of it—the change would have to be imposed on the judges. If I were an old judge, who wore a wig and gown all my life, I should hate to change it. I should be furious if any man proposed it, although it might be most desirable to make a change. It is not an unimportant thing we are discussing. If we were discussing here to-day whether the Supreme

Court should meet in a very imposing building, or in a building which seemed to be unworthy of the nation, we would not think it unimportant to debate the question. I suggest to you that the question of the costume in which the judge gives his decision is of greater importance than the building in which he gives it. Are we to allow very old men, for whom we have the greatest respect, to settle the tradition of this country for centuries, because it will be for centuries if now at a time of revolution when we have a chance we do not create a tradition. Now is our opportunity.

I thank Senator Sir John Keane for his appropriate and friendly quotations from myself. I would like to say that when I talked of this "fool-driven land"—a good many years ago now—I meant that it was fool-driven in certain matters—poetry and the theatre—matters in which I felt I had a greater right to an opinion than I have in politics. Senator Sir John Keane described how a certain judge's cap—a biretta he called it—looked very inappropriate, if worn by a red-haired or a brown-haired man. I would suggest to him that when you see red or brown hair coming from under a grey wig it looks still more inappropriate. [VII, 1039-1058]

> *The amendment was defeated, but the Government at a later date selected robes of office for Irish judges which Yeats had been instrumental in having designed.*

49. COPYRIGHT PROTECTION

February 24, 1927. Industrial and Commercial Property (Protection) Bill.

DR. YEATS: There has been considerable anxiety amongst Irish artists, dramatists and designers, as to how their interests will be affected by this Bill. I think it is right that I should say that I have gone into all the sections which affect their interests, and I think it is a thoroughly good Bill. I think it gives better protection to the Irish designer and dramatist—especially the dramatist—than is given by contemporary English legislation. I had a certain amount of anxiety about one or two details in the Bill as it passed the Dáil, but my anxiety has been removed by Senator Brown's speech. There was one matter on which he did not touch—that is, that the Registrar of Copyrights at Washington has refused to register the copyright of Irish authors. This has caused considerable loss.

I know one Irish author who, acting on legal advice, has published nothing for many months and thereby has suffered considerable financial loss. If you publish in England or Ireland, publication in America has to be practically simultaneous, and if you cannot register your American copyright you may, for the time being, lose it. I know the Government understands this and I know they will make their utmost endeavour, not only to restore our right of registration in the Washington Register, but to make it retrospective so that Irish books published during the interregnum will have registration given them in America. That has been my chief anxiety in connection with this Bill recently, and I know the Government is, as I say, as anxious as I am to put this matter right. I merely speak to urge them to do so quickly because serious loss is being suffered by Irish authors. [VIII, 345]

50. MERRION SQUARE, DUBLIN

March 9, 1927.

MR. BENNETT: I beg to move the Second Reading of the Merrion Square (Dublin) Bill, 1927, the Title of which is as follows:—

A Bill entitled an Act to enable the Commissioners of Merrion Square to convey and transfer to the Trustees of the Irish National War Memorial

Trust the ground within Merrion Square in the City of Dublin and other property vested in the said Commissioners as such; and to provide for the transfer of the said ground to the Right Honourable the Lord Mayor, Aldermen and Burgesses of Dublin from the said Trustees when the same has been laid out as a public park; and for other purposes connected therewith.

.　　　.　　　.　　　.

DR. YEATS: I do not like to speak in this House unless on things I have studied—letters and art. On this occasion, however, I have no choice. I am a resident of Merrion Square. I attended the largely-attended meeting of the residents of Merrion Square to empower the Commissioners to negotiate over this matter. I have no memory for the details or the numbers at that meeting. I do not know how many people were there. I cannot even tell you the date of the meeting. But there were large numbers of residents of the Square at that meeting. I understood, too, that the larger number of those present signed the document necessary. Those of us who are in favour of the opening of the Square to the public—having the Square opened by this memorial scheme—have, I think, certain very strong arguments in our minds. We are all familiar with the argument that there might be a demonstration. We do not believe it, but if we did believe it, it would not influence us. We were not so selfish as to allow our own interests for a few years to interfere with what we believe to be the welfare of the children of Dublin for all time to come.

Very occasionally, perhaps once a year, I go and walk in that Square. We use it very little, and I notice that there are generally children there who have no legal right to be there. The railing is in bad repair and they go in. I should like those children to have a legal right to play in that Square. I should like the Square to be made available for them. Almost every day I go round the waters in Stephen's Green. I know the great delight that that Square and these waters give children. It must enter into their life and memory for ever, and just as I do not think one ought to allow our temporary but possible discomfort for a few years to interfere with the opening of this Square, I do not think we should take too seriously the interests, the fancies or desires of even those admirable men who want a great demonstration upon Armistice Day. Armistice Day will recede. These men will not live for ever. I hope it is not going to become a permanent political demonstration in this country, to be carried on by the children of ex-Servicemen. It will grow less and less every year.

Then you have this question of the monument. I am not greatly interested in the question of the monument one way or the other but I should be very glad indeed if a dignified monument is put up in the Square or wherever the Committee decide, with the names of the men who served in the Great War. That seems to be an entirely worthy and noble ambition. Their great great grandchildren, perhaps a century hence, will go into the Square and point out the names of their ancestors upon that monument. That is a different thing from the annual demonstration of thousands in the midst of the city. I was very much surprised by something in Senator Sir Bryan Mahon's speech. He said that no matter what these ex-Servicemen were told to do they would if they preferred it, go and demonstrate in the middle of Merrion Square. Now 100,000 men do not go and demonstrate anywhere without being organised. He meant that there are ex-Servicemen who are prepared to demonstrate against the orders of their own leaders because I refuse to believe that Senator Sir Bryan Mahon and Senator Sir William Hickie would order them to demonstrate against the direction of the city and of the Government in the midst of Merrion Square. No, they would rather order them to go to the replica of the Cenotaph, an exact replica of the one in Whitehall, which I understand the promoters of this measure are quite prepared to erect in the Phoenix Park. They would, as loyal citizens, not annoy the citizens in this way, but Senator Sir Bryan Mahon thinks that there are men who will organise against that, against their own leaders and the State, will hold their own memorial service and trample down the flowers in the midst of the Square. I am sorry to say that I cannot believe Senator Sir Bryan Mahon.

I think he is misrepresenting the ex-Servicemen. I do not think there are such men amongst them. I think he himself has been carried away by the propaganda against this memorial. I have heard no argument against it from any resident of Merrion Square except, precisely, this argument that men would demonstrate in the Square and destroy the place, make a noise, annoy the inhabitants of the Square and make them uncomfortable. I support the scheme very heartily because I do not believe that in 100 years any monument erected now will be very important. Wellington Monument is not in a sense a very important monument. But I believe in 100 years the Square will be there if this scheme is carried out for the health of the Dublin children and the delight of all the citizens. [VIII, 444-46]

51. COPYRIGHT PROTECTION

March 11, 1927. Industrial and Commercial Property (Protection) Bill.

MR. BROWN: I beg to move amendment 24:—

Section 154.

(1) Subject to the provisions of this Act, copyright shall subsist in Saorstat Eireann for the term hereinafter mentioned in every original literary, dramatic, musical, and artistic work, if—

(a) in the case of a published work, the work was first published within Saorstat Eireann or a part of the British dominions to which the benefit of this Part of this Act extends; and . . .

(2) . . .

(a) to produce, reproduce, perform, or publish any translation of the work; . . .

MR. CUMMINS: The object of the amendment primarily is to make Dublin what it once was—a great centre of printing, one of the leading centres, perhaps, in the British Isles, when it turned out a quality of work equal to any of its kind. . . . That is one of the objects of the amendment—to promote and encourage the printing trade in Dublin. Another object, of course, is that incidentally you give employment to a very large number of the members of the trade, who are at present largely unemployed.

DR. YEATS: I think I may, perhaps, allay some of the feelings of the Senators by demonstrating, as I shall, that the proposal of Senator Cummins is entirely absurd and unworkable. Last Monday evening a very distinguished scholar came to see me. He has devoted his life to editing texts in Middle and Old Irish. He told me that scholars and members of learned societies were alarmed. He began by pointing out to me that much has been done lately in phonetics in the vernacular, that is to say, taking down Irish dialects. It is very important work, and is an attempt to record the pronunciation of the various dialects of Ireland. They are not taken down in any alphabet of any country, but in a special set of symbols. No Irish publisher possesses those symbols. The result is that those books, recording the Irish dialect, are printed in Copenhagen and Germany. He pointed out to me that if this were passed certain scholars who have done this work, who are not citizens of the Saorstat, would possess the copyright of their work. Those who are citizens of the Saorstat would possess it in every country except their own. He then went on to point out to me that practically all works of learning are produced by certain Presses which are subvented [*sic*] from universities.

There is no publisher in Ireland who will accept or could accept such books. These books are brought to the University Press in Cambridge or the Clarendon Press in Oxford, or rather to the publishing houses which take their name from these Presses. These books pay the authors practically nothing at all. The learned man is satisfied merely that his scholarship should be given to the world. If you pass this law these men will have copyright in every country except their own. I should add further that in publishing a work of this kind it is not only necessary to find the publisher who will take your work and pay for the printing, but it is desirable to find the publisher who has that very expensive thing—a highly-trained "reader to the press." No Irish publisher possesses it, as I know to my cost, but it is of enormous importance when dealing with works of learning. It may be said that as these learned men cannot be published except by subventioned presses, no matter what law you pass, they will not be printed in Ireland; that they should be left out of the argument.

We are thinking of the future. This is an ill-educated country. We all hope that will change. You are dealing with works 50 years after the death of the author. Such copyright may be all he has to leave to his children; some of these books, years and years hence, may be of considerable value. There are other works of scholarship which are of immediate value. At the Cambridge University Press are published great universal histories. One, a modern history, is finished. The Ancient History and Medieval History are unfinished. These are the works of a great many different scholars. One scholar's work may run into 300 pages. The work of these texts is done by University scholars. Those are men who cannot change their citizenship. Those men who have done this work cannot set up British citizenship. At once on the publication of this great universal history an Irish publisher can take 300 pages out, perhaps, the research of a man's life, and publish it here. Probably when this many-volumed ancient history is completed it may contain a large section on Early Ireland, hundreds of pages that could be taken out immediately and published in this country.

It is quite obvious that no Irish author, no matter how patriotic, could persuade publishers of these universal histories to print in Ireland. They are always printed in certain University Presses which have a subvention from the university. I will give you another example. Many Irish scholars have done work on the Encyclopedia Britannica. They cannot very well persuade publishers of the Encyclopedia Britannica to print in Ireland.

MRS. WYSE-POWER: They are not publishers. They are only employed to do the work.

DR. YEATS: I do not understand the point of that. The editors of the Encyclopedia will get their lives of O'Connell, of Burke, and of Parnell from Irish writers. Those authors will not succeed in inducing the great Encyclopedia Britannica Company to change their whole habits of printing and print in Ireland. The idea is absurd. The Irish publisher can extract these lives of O'Connell, Burke and Parnell, containing the latest information on their subjects, and can publish them here, and what is more there is at present no law whatever which can prevent him sending them to England. Anyone can write from England, as they write at present to an Irish bookseller, and ask for such a book. At present there is no machinery to stop these books from going to England. What will happen is, Irish scholars will not be employed because they have only an impaired copyright to offer. I am sure no one in this House wishes to do this great injury to Irish scholars. That, I think, we are agreed to.

I dare say, however, when they come to considering a creative writer they are in a different sphere. There is the idea that a creative writer is making a great deal of money. They have in their imagination that he is. A few are singularly wealthy men—Mr. George Bernard Shaw, Mr. Arnold Bennett, and Mr. H. G. Wells. These men are exceptional. No doubt they can dictate to their publishers and tell them where they are to print. If the publisher does not agree to print wherever they dictate they can say: "I will go to another publisher." Remember an old couplet of the eighteenth century. It is not far out when you go over in your own mind the lives of men whose work has become immortal. It is:

> "Seven Grecian cities fought for Homer dead,
> Through which the living Homer begged his bread."

Very few authors win success before they reach forty years of age. Very few authors, no matter what their later careers, are in a position to change their publishers or dictate to their publishers. One young Irish novelist of today has, I know, made an agreement for a term of years. His publisher pays him so much a year and he gives him all he produces. That man loses his copyright unless he declares himself a British citizen. You are compelling export of your authors. Perhaps I might be a little personal. At the start I wish to say that I have had a very smooth and easy career. I make no complaint whatever. I was 45 before I ever earned from my books or by serial publication of their contents, as much as the £4 a week earned by Irish printers. During the last four or five years of that time I was able to enlarge my income by lecturing. I was not in a position to change my publisher. My publisher was Mr. A. H. Bullen. He had a rather famous Press—The Shakespeare Head Press. I cannot see myself going to Mr. A. H. Bullen, who had given me beautifully printed books, and who took me at a time another publisher refused me, and saying: "I shall withdraw unless you change your printers." Even much more celebrated men than I am have had the same experience even towards the end of their lives. Robert Browning told Lady Gregory that he would have made more money at any profession, even making matches. He was not in a position to change his publisher. Do you think it is a dignified position for a nation to say: "You will not have copyright in Ireland unless you can cajole your publisher; speak smooth to him?" Cajole! that is what you want authors to do. You are passing a law of cajolery.

I notice another result to which I wish to draw your attention. No Irish author can serialise his work in the English Press or newspaper and keep his copyright. No author, I think, however successful, who is dependent on his work for a living can afford to give up serialising his work in the English press. Just as you have no Irish publishers prepared to take Irish authors' work, you have no Irish magazines or Irish newspapers prepared at their own expense to undertake the serialising of authors' work, and give anything like adequate pay for it; if they could pay for it at all. One Irish author—I will not mention names—a very celebrated woman, has at this moment ready for publication an autobiography covering many years and dealing with many things and personalities important in Irish history. It deals also with many great English, social and political questions. That autobiography will be serialised in the English Press. If this law is passed it will be immediately pirated by the Irish Press, which will not pay a penny to the author. It will also be pirated in book form. You cannot compel an English newspaper or review to print in Ireland for the sake of one contribution. It would be preposterous. So far as the copyright of books is concerned I do not suppose it personally will affect me. I have done the bulk of my work. Can I go to my publisher and say: "I want you to print in Ireland"? If he says "No," what am I to do? He has all my works, my collected edition: I lose heavily if I detach my work from that uniform edition, and have broken faith with those who purchased that edition on the understanding that it is to be a genuine collected edition. Cajolery! This great State is going to pass a law by which people are to be cajoled to do what it wants. I will not leave this country because you appropriate my books, the few I have to write. If you made it impossible for me or any Irish author to serialise our work our income would suffer. I shall not leave this country, but shall move to the border, and I assure you I shall become exceedingly eloquent if I do.

There is no reason in the world why this town should not become a centre of printing and publishing. I am not speaking in entire ignorance. I have some little experience. Some 25 years ago at the establishment of the Abbey Theatre I became editor of the Cuala Press. It is a hand press which employs several Irish printers all the year round. Nearly all my first editions have been printed by that Press. The first editions of a great many writers were printed there. As it is now the longest-established hand press in these islands, I have a right to say we have succeeded. There is no reason why what we have done in a small way cannot be done by this country on a large scale. If you are to do it on a large scale you must do the work as well and as cheaply as it is done elsewhere. There is a misunderstanding about printing. The artisan prints well. He seldom does bad work. The bad work that prevents your publishers and printers succeeding is done because they have not men of taste to select type, arrange proper proportions, margins, binding and the other necessaries of well-turned-out books.

You can make a great centre of publishing and printing here, because Ireland has a good literary prestige in the world now. But, if you got all the Irish authors in the world to publish here they would not be, in themselves, sufficient in number to make it a great publishing centre. If you are going to make it even a paying centre for printing and publishing, apart from making it a great centre, you must keep the goodwill of the publishers of the world, and you must keep the goodwill of the men of letters of the world. You will certainly not do so by what will be considered all over Europe as pirating. The educated opinion of Europe sees no difference between the property in a book and the property in an article of manufacture. You would not think of confiscating Jacob's biscuits because the tin in which they are put up was not made in Ireland. That is the educated opinion of Europe.

I have here a document to which I would like to draw the attention of those interested in Irish publishing. Some time ago a book by an Irish author was printed in America. I have a protest signed by 150 men, whose names are those of men of great eminence all over Europe. I will mention some of these names. They are from all countries.

Germany is represented by that man often described as the greatest mathematician and man of science of our day—Einstein. There are appended the names of other celebrated German authors. Russia is represented by the president of the famous Russian academy of letters. Spain is represented by the President of the Spanish Academy, Azarin; the most celebrated of her dramatists, Benavente, and the great Catholic philosopher, Miguel de Unamuno. Italy is represented by her Minister of Education, Giovanni Gentile, who is also a very great philosopher, and who, it may be of interest to some Senators to know, has organised the entire education of Italy in a way of far greater perfection than any educational system of Europe. It may be also well to know that he has restored religious education to the schools. Austria is represented by Hofmannsthal, a very great dramatist and poet. Belgium is represented by the dramatist, Maurice Maeterlinck, and France is represented by various members of the French Academy of great eminence. England is represented by a great many names, such as John Galsworthy and Bertrand Russell.

That appeal is not merely an appeal to American opinion to condemn piracy; it is an appeal to advertisers to withdraw advertisements from the publisher who has committed this act of piracy. Do you think Irish publishing houses will flourish if they carry on piracy of that kind? No, decidedly not. The world has become sensitive in recent years on the question of literary copyright, because it involves the prestige of men of letters in all countries. You can only make a successful publishing or printing house here if you keep the goodwill of publishers and the goodwill of men of letters.

.   .   .   .

COL. MOORE: I had every wish to vote in favour of the amendment, but I must confess that after hearing Senator Yeats I have been completely changed in my opinion. I do not think it would be right or proper in the circumstances to assent to the conditions complained of. [VIII, 599-608]

Amendment withdrawn by leave.

52. MERRION SQUARE, DUBLIN

April 7, 1927. Merrion Square (Dublin) Bill.

DR. YEATS: I want to ask a question of the promoters of the Bill. The wisdom of the decision of the Dáil has been very much discussed, and I think it would help the community to give an enlightened decision if my question were answered. If this Bill passed, the people of Dublin would have come into possession of Merrion Square as a park for ever. I understand that the trustees of the Pembroke Estate will in twelve years be at liberty to sell Merrion Square as a building site. It is inconceivable that the Dublin Commissioners should desire or, if they could prevent it, should permit that great open space to be built over. I have heard, however, a very high sum mentioned as the price the Commissioners will have to pay for Merrion Square if they have to buy it. There is no doubt that they would have to pay for its building value. I would be obliged if you, sir, would permit Senator Jameson, who is perhaps best informed as to the fact, to reply to my question.

MR. JAMESON: I have only information of a very casual kind, and I do not know that the valuation could be relied on very accurately. I think I am certainly understating the figures when I say that twelve years hence, with a building scheme attached to it, the site should be worth anything from £50,000 to £100,000. [VIII, 722]

53. COPYRIGHT PROTECTION

May 4, 1927. Industrial and Commercial Property (Protection) Bill.

DR. YEATS: I would like if the Minister would be able to deal with the difficulty that I put before him, about making some arrangements by which we would be able to confer copyright on American works excluded under our present arrangement, in order to obtain copyright in the interregnum. I have been away in connection with the Lane pictures and I was not able to go into the matter.

MR. MCGILLIGAN: As I explained, in so far as our relations depend, anything we agree about can be adjusted under Section 176. In other words, this Order can be made applicable under certain conditions to America. The difficulty about the interregnum period does not lie with us. It lies in the legislation of the United States. The rule we have seems to forbid the giving of any retroactive effect. The Order made is the Order which will be enforced here under Section 176 in the interregnum period to which the section refers. We would have no difficulty with it, but under the existing legislation it is doubtful if the American President could make his Order have retrospective effect. As far as we can arrange things on this side this arrangement will be made. [VIII, 1107]

54. COPYRIGHT PROTECTION

May 4, 1927. Industrial and Commercial Property (Protection) Bill (Resumed).

MR. DOWDALL: . . . This matter was dealt with at considerable length on the Committee Stage. We were told in the Press and by Senator Yeats at considerable length that this was an illiterate country in which no one reads. He assured us he would go to the Border if this amendment were carried. If that is true, what is the object of proposing this amendment? A good many people may read unknown to those who are opposing the amendment. . . .

. . . .

DR. YEATS: I am in great difficulty. I discussed all this fully on the Committee Stage, but it seems I shall have to discuss it again and bore the House very much. I asked Senator Brown whether he thought I could omit my discussion of it and he thinks the matter of such importance that I must re-discuss the whole thing again.

. . . .

MR. CUMMINS: The object that Senator Dowdall's amendment would secure is that Irish authors resident in Ireland should before they secure copyright in their own country have at least the book printed in this country. . . . There are eminent men in various countries, many eminent men in literature, eminent men in science, eminent men in Christian life, and I shall leave it to this House to judge which is the greater eminence, Christian eminence or the eminence that would destroy all semblance of Christianity on the face of the earth? . . .

On the last occasion that this matter was discussed, I ploughed a very lonely furrow here. The soil was very difficult in which to steer my horses. Senator Yeats made it still more difficult. He made a very violent onslaught upon all things Irish.

DR. YEATS: I did not.

MR. CUMMINS: Possibly I should not say a violent onslaught, but he subjected them to severe criticism, and, in fact, we were branded almost as an illiterate nation, not worth printing for. He drew a pathetic picture of an author to publish whose book various attempts were made in certain countries. I shall not name the author. Neither did Senator Yeats name the author, and I am glad because of the delicacy and the sensitiveness—

DR. YEATS: James Joyce.

MR. CUMMINS: —and the literary taste of the people of this country, that he did not name the author upon whose behalf a petition was signed by the highbrows—

DR. YEATS: By 150 of the most eminent men in Europe.

MR. CUMMINS: By the most eminent men in Europe, if he prefers the title. The picture was drawn to play upon the feelings of members of this House to such an extent that he secured the object he was aiming at. . . . I would like to ask Senator Yeats to give us the history of the book which he spoke of in such feeling terms on the last occasion. I would ask him is it true that the British Post Office authorities have really refused to send this book through their channels, that it has been actually refused in America, that the indelicacy and the outrageous character of that book were of such a nature that it would not be permitted to go through the ordinary channels of delivery in any Christian country? The Senator tells us that this appeal is sufficiently strong to influence this House, but if this House is influenced by the appeal, it will be a surprise for the gods.

DR. GOGARTY: Is this not rather beside the point?

MR. CUMMINS: . . . The Senator made a threat that if he did not succeed in carrying his negative proposal he would cross the Border.

AN CATHAOIRLEACH: The Senator to whom you are referring has not spoken or intervened in this debate at all. I think perhaps it is a little bit out of order to be referring back to parts of a speech delivered on a former occasion.

MR. CUMMINS: I anticipate that the Senator will speak.

AN CATHAOIRLEACH: Perhaps he will now. You want him to stand on the tail of your coat.

DR. YEATS: I think on the whole I shall speak. I think the Senator is quite correct. I do not like it to be supposed that I did not mention the name of James Joyce because the book was a discredit to him. I did not mention the name, because it had nothing to do with the issue. Some 150 of the most eminent men in Europe signed the protest against the mutilation and piracy of James Joyce's book in America. Some of these men sincerely admired that book and thought it a very great book. Some of those who signed the protest did not admire it at all and signed it simply because of the copyright issue. I know of one case, certainly, where a very eminent person disapproved greatly of the book, but his signature was given because of the copyright issue. American publishers had a perfect right to print that book according to the law, because it was not copyright in America. Reputable American publishers do not so pirate work. There are more or less disreputable publishers who do. There is a publisher called Roothe who pirated this book of James Joyce. I am not going to defend James Joyce. It is a very difficult question. Has the Senator ever looked into Rabelais? Rabelais is looked upon as one of the greatest masters of the past, and what is to be said of James Joyce may be said of Rabelais.

I would point out to the Senator that attached to this petition is the name of Gentile, the Italian Minister of Education, who has restored religious teaching to the schools in Italy. Another who signed this was the great Catholic philosopher of Spain, Unamuno. Does he think, leaving aside these men of special religious achievement, that there is nothing to be said for a book or a man testified to by the head of the Spanish Academy, the President of the famous Russian Academy of Letters, by various members of the French Academy of great eminence, and by the greatest living mathematician, Einstein? When I heard the Senator put up Irish opinions as against these, as certainly and definitely right, then I was inclined to believe this was an illiterate nation. These things cannot be settled as easily as that. I do not know whether Joyce's "Ulysses" is a great work of literature. I have puzzled a great deal over that question.

AN CATHAOIRLEACH: We are travelling too far. We are not discussing this book.

DR. YEATS: All I will say is that it is the work of an heroic mind. I think Senator Dowdall acted without due thought in bringing forward this amendment. I was visited by an eminent Irish scholar who asked me to urge the House to throw out this printing clause in the interests of Irish scholarship, very largely in the interests of Irish Gaelic scholarship. Certain Irish books on phonetics are printed in Copenhagen and Germany because the characters do not exist in any Irish printing office. If this clause were passed, then in the case of those books written by Irishmen those firms would lose their Irish copyright.

He then however passed on to a very much more serious thing. Most of the work of scholarship has to be published at certain great presses which are subventioned, the Clarendon Press at Oxford and the University Press at Cambridge. We may take it that no Irish printer or publisher would deal with that kind of scholarship at all, for such works have a very small immediate sale. The sale is so small that it would not pay an Irish publisher to print those works without a subvention from the State or the University. But we are all thinking of the future. We are hoping that in the course of the next twenty or thirty years a very considerable reading public will grow up in this country.

You are dealing with property which lasts not only for the lifetime of the author but for fifty years after his death. Some of the work of the scholars may be valuable property which they should have the right to leave to their children. If you pass this law you will pass a law which will injure Irish scholars. You will deprive those scholars of a copyright which may grow to be of a great monetary value. We differ from Canada because in Canada there is a publishing centre and wealthy Universities. I think there are endowed University presses there. Furthermore, there is nothing in Canada like the great Irish republic of Letters which has grown up here for two centuries. One of the few means by which an Irish scholar can make money is by contributing to certain great collective publications like the universal histories now being published at the Cambridge Press. There are three great universal histories, ancient, modern and mediaeval, being published in many volumes by that Press. In those volumes portions are by separate scholars. Some are by Irish scholars. There is no possibility of getting those printed in Ireland. An Irish publisher could take out a whole section of one of those books dealing with Ireland and pirate it here. If there were no piracy then the Senator's printing clause would be inoperative. It is a clause which the whole world will regard as an incitement to piracy. There are also such compilations as the "Dictionary of National Biography," and the "Encyclopaedia Britannica." Several of our Irish scholars have worked on these for many years.

There are always new editions. Universal histories will always be produced. The whole publishing and printing system by which Irish scholars live will be upset not only in dealing with these great compilations but in connection with another side of the question which Senator Dowdall has not thought of. If his final amendment down on the Paper is carried no Irish writer will be able to serialise his work in England. A young novelist will not be able to publish his stories in the "Windsor" or "Pall Mall" magazines. I have mentioned a case in which an eminent Irish writer has just finished an important autobiography which in the ordinary course of events would be published in an English newspaper.

That work could be pirated here. The Irish newspapers might take out large sections. What would happen to an Irish author? He sends a story to the "Windsor Magazine." The "Windsor Magazine" says: "No, we cannot publish it; you are a citizen of the Free State." Someone in Ireland would pirate the story and then the right Senator Dowdall proposes to confer upon that person could exclude the "Windsor Magazine" from Ireland. Not only are you giving the Irish publisher the right to pirate sections from the magazines, newspapers, the great universal histories, the "Dictionary of National Biography," and "Encyclopaedia Britannica," but you are going to give him the right to exclude from Ireland these publications. The thing is laughable. A sane man should not give two minutes' thought to the amendment. What are you going to gain in the end? If you have all the Irish writers that exist printing here in Dublin they are not sufficient to keep your printing presses busy for half a year.

MR. DOWDALL: What is your authority for saying that?

DR. YEATS: I cannot give statistics. I know pretty well who the Irish authors are whose works have some value in the market. They are not very numerous. If you get them all you cannot make a successful centre of printing in Ireland unless you get English publishers to print here. At this moment one of the Irish printers is successfully printing a number of popular novels for an English publisher. What will happen when you commit the first conspicuous act of piracy? There is a body called the Publishers' Association and another the Society of Authors. What will happen will be on a very much larger scale than what happened in the case of that pirated book in America when 150 authors protested not only to American sentiment but also made an appeal to American publishers to withdraw advertisements from a particular journal. What will happen will be far greater because action will come through the English Publishers' Association and the Society of Authors. Your entire printing will be snuffed out and you will outrage the opinion of the world as Canada has not, because you will be the first

European nation to break in upon the accord of Europe on the subject of intellectual property.

America is moving towards the European position. As late as thirty years ago there was practically no copyright in America. The works of the most eminent writers, such as Dickens and Thackeray, were pirated. It was a world scandal. Then gradually the finer tastes of America were able to assert themselves and the Copyright Act was passed. No educated American looks upon that as final, but that it is simply moving towards the European position. Naturally, perhaps, Canada adopted the same law, which deals not only with Canadian but with American citizens. You will be very different. You will not be moving from a condition of piracy, but towards it, and you will bring upon your head an amount of obloquy of which you have no idea. I do not want to close with what the Senator calls "negation." Ireland is now, intellectually, in the position Edinburgh was at the beginning of the nineteenth century. Gradually Edinburgh became a great centre of publishing and printing. Edinburgh had great intellectual prestige. We have given you intellectual prestige. It will be your fault if you do not make Dublin a great centre of printing, but you will not make it a great centre of printing unless you retain the goodwill of the publishers and writers of England and the British Empire. [IX, 1115-19]

After further discussion amendment put and negatived.

55. SENATE MEMBERSHIP

July 18, 1928. Constitution (Amendment No. 6) Bill, 1928. On the process of electing members to the Senate.

DR. YEATS: I think we should not lose sight of the simple fact that it is more desirable and more important to have able men in this

House than to get representative men into this House. Looking down the list of Senators who will be going up for re-election—I am not one of them—I am certain that the ablest men on that list stand a better opportunity of returning to this House if this Bill be passed, than they would stand if the Bill be not passed. [X, 1097]

Bill passed.

Appendix I

THE NOBEL PRIZE: CONGRATULATIONS TO SENATOR YEATS

On the 15th of November, 1923, Yeats was awarded the Nobel Prize for Literature. Senator Oliver Gogarty extended the formal congratulations of the Senate to Yeats as follows, on November 28:

DR. OLIVER GOGARTY: I move—

"that the Senate congratulates Senator Yeats on his winning of the Nobel Prize for Literature; and thanks him for the recognition which the nation has gained, as a prominent contributor to the world's culture, through his success."

I hope that it will be as welcome and as grateful a task to the members of the House to pass this motion of congratulation as it is to me to propose it. To my mind, since the Treaty the award of the Nobel Prize to Senator Yeats is the most significant thing that has befallen this country, and I will try to explain the reason. There would be great room for misconception as regards the value of the Arts, and I suppose in no other subject has so much nonsense been spoken as on that very matter. There are two ways of regarding artistic work: one is the individual. A man may have a certain idiosyncrasy which is utterly worthless, or a man may have an output of work which is thoroughly valuable to the nation as regards its social angle, and it is, on that, I think, that the merit lies with Senator Yeats, because for over twenty-five years he set his face sternly against any false enthusiasm or idealism, or any attempt to make poetry into patriotism, and he has invited and sustained a great deal of unpopularity. But on no occasion has he ever written tawdry poetry in order to make his purse heavier. When a detached and impartial nation, and a nation with discrimination such as the highly educated Swedes have, selected Senator Yeats for such an award, above and in spite of the recommendation of the Literary Committee of Great Britain, and in view of the immense body of literature, both historical and epic, at present in existence in France and Germany, and selected him from a race that hitherto had not been accepted into the comity of nations, at any rate socially, is an honour we ought to show our awareness of by making our congratulation to him take the form of Senatorial recognition.

When we look back on the history of civilization, when we survey rapidly the contributions to human culture which the different races of the world have made, one or two names, or perhaps three only, are outstanding. In Greece we all know there are names outstanding, such as Plato and Aristotle. In Italy, Virgil and Dante, and coming down to modern times, men like Marconi and Mussolini. In the 18th century, we had Berkeley, Swift, and Molyneux. We can see the aridness of the nations which have no outstanding men. I am not making any geographical references to our country, but to such places as Persia, where there are no outstanding names. What is the meaning of these outstanding names? The meaning is that it is by men such as they that our civilisation is assessed. Our civilisation will be assessed on the name of Senator Yeats. Coming at a time when there was a regular wave of destruction, hatred of beauty, a crushing out of perfection, and a blindness to the national ideal in this country, it is a very happy and welcome thing. True, perhaps, it was only led by a few ferocious and home-breaking old harridans, but the very fact that it was put forward as a political program makes one anxious as to the sanity of some. One danger to the country is the large body who have never been made in any way aware of the enormity of the vote. Until we have instructed our franchise-bearers there will always be the danger that there may be a stampeding of people who are sufficiently removed from insanity in enthusiasm for destruction.

AN CATHAOIRLEACH: Do not forget the text of your motion.

DR. GOGARTY: I am showing the extreme gratitude that the House should bear to Senator Yeats, and the fact that all great art must have a national significance, but I will take up the time of the House no longer.

AN CATHAOIRLEACH: . . . [it is] a fitting recognition of his great literary gifts, but we take the greater pride in it on account of the courage and patriotism which induced him twelve months ago to cast in his lot with his own people here at home, under conditions which were then very critical and called for the exercise of great moral courage, and not only for doing that but also for placing his very great gifts at the service of the Senate. [II, 156-60 *passim*]

Appendix II

DIVORCE: AN UNDELIVERED SPEECH

Early in March, 1925, Yeats sent the following version of his Divorce Speech and an accompanying note to George Russell, editor of The Irish Statesman: *"Expecting a debate upon the problem of Divorce in the Senate on March 4, I had made notes for a speech. As the Message from the Dáil was ruled out of order, debate was impossible. As I think that whoever can should help to inform public opinion before the matter comes round again, I send you my notes."*

I SHALL vote against the resolution sent up to us by the Dáil, not because I am interested in the subject of divorce, but because I consider the resolution an act of aggression. We have the right to assume—it was indeed declared in so many words at a meeting of the Catholic Truth Society—that no Catholic would avail himself of opportunities for divorce; and President Cosgrave has before him the example of Quebec, where, though the proportion of Catholics is greater than in Ireland, facilities of divorce are permitted to the minority, but he had preferred to impose his Catholic convictions upon members of the Church of Ireland and upon men of no church.

I know that at the present stage of the discussion a large part of the Irish public, perhaps a majority, supports him, and I do not doubt the sincerity of that support—the sincerity that has heard only one side is invariably without flaw—and I have no doubt even that if he and they possessed the power they would legislate with the same confidence for Turks, Buddhists and followers of Confucius. It is an impressive spectacle, so quixotically impressive, indeed, that one has to seek its like in Mediaeval Spain. I wonder, however, if President Cosgrave and his supporters have calculated the cost—but no, I am wrong to wonder that, for such enthusiasm does not calculate the cost.

This country has declared through every vehicle of expression known to it that it desires union with the North of Ireland, even that it will never be properly a nation till that union has been achieved, and it knows that it cannot bring that union about by force. It must convince the Ulster Protestants that if they join themselves to us they will not suffer injustice. They can be won, not now, but in a generation, but they cannot be won if you insist that the Catholic conscience alone must dominate the public life of Ireland. The Catholic Church fought for years against the Unity of Italy, and even invited recruits from this country to help it in that fight, and though it had the highest motives history has condemned it, and now it is about to fight against the Unity of Ireland.

But there is another cost which I will remind you of, though I am sure the Irish Bishops and President Cosgrave, whether they have calculated it or not, are prepared to pay it, and I shall speak of it, not to influence them, but because various journalists have charged those who favour divorce with advocating sexual immorality. The price that you pay for indissoluble marriage is a public opinion that will tolerate illegal relations between the sexes. Sometime ago I was talking to an Italian of an illustrious Catholic house, from which have come cardinals and, I believe, one Pope, and he spoke of what he considered the extreme harshness of American public opinion to illicit relations between the sexes, and explained it by the ease of divorce in America, which made such relations seem inexcusable. He thought that Italy was wiser, and said that the indissoluble marriage of Italy, of which he approved, caused great tolerance towards such relations. In describing Italy, he described, I think, every country where marriage has been indissoluble, Spain,

France of the eighteenth century, and all mediaeval Europe. I will call Balzac as evidence, and not merely because he was the greatest of French novelists, but because he prided himself in recording the France of his own day. He was writing about aristocratic France which, though divorce was permitted since the French Revolution, was ardently Catholic, and did not recognise the laws of the Revolution. One of the most charming of his heroines is about to be married, and her mother takes her aside that she may speak these words: "Remember, my child, that if you love your husband that is the most fortunate of all things, but if you do not you will no doubt take a lover. All I say to you is, do nothing against the family." Then Balzac uses these remarkable words: "She went to the altar with the words of that noble woman ringing in her ears."

I have just read the book in which my friend Mr. Chesterton puts the Catholic case with so much ability, and I find nothing incompatible with the advice of that French mother; he is too wise an advocate of indissoluble marriage not to base it upon the family and the family only. It is a protection to the family, a protection to the children, or it is believed to be so, and its advocates think that the price is worth paying.

I am certainly not going to reason against that conviction, I certainly do not think that I have anything to say that can affect an issue that has been debated by men of the greatest sincerity and intellect for generations. I shall merely put another point of view, that we may understand each other the better, a point of view which is held with passion by men who follow the teachings of some Church that is not under Rome, or like myself, believe as little in an infallible book as an infallible church. For a long time there has been a religious truce in Ireland, men like myself have kept silent about all those matters that divide one religion from another, but President Cosgrave has broken that truce, and I will avail myself of the freedom he has given me. Marriage is not to us a Sacrament, but, upon the other hand, the love of man and woman, and the inseparable physical desire, are sacred. This conviction has come to us through ancient philosophy and modern literature, and it seems to us a most sacrilegious thing to persuade two people who hate one another because of some unforgettable wrong, to live together, and it is to us no remedy to permit them to part if neither can remarry. We know that means the formation of ties which are commonly unhappy because transitory, and immoral because separated from the rest of life, and which, if there are children, may send the wrong into the future. We believe, too, that where such ties are not formed the emotions and therefore the spiritual life may be perverted and starved.

The Church of Ireland permits the remarriage of such persons, and the head of the Church of England has accepted the present Divorce Law of England. Neither would, perhaps, extend that law, but it will be extended in the future, for no nation which dates its public life from the Reformation will permanently compel a man or woman to remain solitary if husband or wife has been condemned to life-long imprisonment or has been certified as an incurable lunatic. We do not think that children brought up in a house of hatred, where the parents quarrel perpetually, are the better for it, and we are certain that a stepmother is better than no mother, even if the real mother is but in gaol or mad or bad beyond reformation, or estranged beyond recall, and we put our faith in human nature, and think that if you give men good education you can trust their intellects and their consciences without making rules that seem to us arbitrary. Some rules there have to be, for we live together in corporate society, but they are matters of practical convenience, and we think that they should be made by statesmen and not by a celibate clergy, however patriotic or public-spirited.

I do not think that my words will influence a single vote here, nor am I thinking of this House, I am thinking only of a quarrel which I perceive is about to commence. Fanaticism having won this victory, and I see nothing that can prevent it unless it be proved to have overstepped the law, will make other attempts upon the liberty of minorities. I want those minorities to resist, and their resistance may do an overwhelming service to this country, they may become the centre of its creative intellect and the pivot of its unity. For the last hundred years

Irish Nationalism has had to fight against England, and that fight has helped Fanaticism, for we had to welcome everything that gave Ireland emotional energy, and had little use for intelligence so far as the mass of the people were concerned, for we had to hurl them against an alien power. The basis of Irish nationalism has now shifted, and much that once helped us is now injurious, for we can no longer do anything by fighting, we must persuade, and to persuade we must become a modern, tolerant, liberal nation. I want everything discussed, I want to get rid of the old exaggerated tact and caution. As a people we are superficial, our Press provincial and trivial, because as yet we have not considered any of those great political and religious questions which raise some fundamental issues and have disturbed Europe for generations. It must depend upon a small minority which is content to remain a minority for a generation to insist on those questions being discussed. Let us use the weapons that have been put into our hands.

From The Irish Statesman, *March 14, 1925, 8-10.*

Appendix III

IRISH COINAGE

"What We Did or Tried to Do," by W. B. Yeats, *Chairman of the Committee.*

I

As THE most famous and beautiful coins are the coins of the Greek Colonies, especially of those in Sicily, we decided to send photographs of some of these, and one coin of Carthage, to our selected artists, and to ask them, as far as possible, to take them as a model. But the Greek coins had two advantages that ours could not have, one side need not balance the other, and either could be stamped in high relief, whereas ours must pitch and spin to please the gambler, and pack into rolls to please the banker.

II

We asked advice as to symbols, and were recommended by the public: round towers, wolf hounds, shamrocks, single or in wreaths, and the Treaty Stone of Limerick; and advised by the Society of Antiquaries to avoid patriotic emblems altogether, for even the shamrock emblem was not a hundred years old. We would have avoided them in any case, for we had to choose such forms as permit an artist to display all his capacity for design and expression, and as Ireland is the first modern

State to design an entire coinage, not one coin now and another years later, as old dies wear out or the public changes its taste, it seemed best to give the coins some relation to one another. The most beautiful Greek coins are those that represent some god or goddess, as a boy or girl, or those that represent animals or some simple object like a wheat-ear. Those beautiful forms, when they are re-named Hibernia or Liberty, would grow empty and academic, and the wheat-ear had been adopted by several modern nations. If we decided upon birds and beasts, the artist, the experience of centuries has shown, might achieve a masterpiece, and might, or so it seemed to us, please those that would look longer at each coin than anybody else, artists and children. Besides, what better symbols could we find for this horse-riding, salmon-fishing, cattle-raising country?

III

We might have chosen figures from the history of Ireland, saints or national leaders, but a decision of the Executive Council excluded modern men, and no portraits have come down to us of St. Brigid or King Brian. The artist, to escape academical convention, would have invented a characteristic but unrecognisable head. I have before me a Swedish silver coin and a Swedish bronze medal, both masterly, that display the head of their mediaeval King, Gustavus Vasa. But those marked features were as familiar to the people as the incidents of his life, the theme of two famous plays. But even had we such a figure a modern artist might prefer not to suggest some existing knowledge, but to create new beauty by an arrangement of lines.

IV

But how should the Government choose its artists? What advice should we give? It should reject a competition open to everybody. No good artist would spend day after day designing, and perhaps get nothing by it. There should be but a few competitors, and whether a man's work were chosen or not he should be paid something, and he should know, that he might have some guarantee of our intelligence, against whom he competed. We thought seven would be enough, and that of these three should be Irish. We had hoped to persuade Charles Shannon, a master of design, whose impressive caps and robes the Benchers of the King's Inn had rejected in favour of wig and gown, to make one of these, but he refused, and that left us two Dublin sculptors of repute, Albert Power and Oliver Sheppard, and Jerome Connor arrived lately from New York. Before choosing the other four we collected examples of modern coinage with the help of various Embassies or of our friends. When we found anything to admire—the Italian coin with the wheat-ear or that with the Fascist emblem; the silver Swedish coin with the head of Gustavus Vasa; the American bison coin—we found out the artist's name and asked for other specimens of his work, if we did not know it already. We also examined the work of various medallists, and, much as we admired the silver Gustavus Vasa, we preferred a bronze Gustavus Vasa by the great Swedish sculptor Carl Milles. Carl Milles and Ivan Mestrovic, sculptor and medallist, have expressed in their work a violent rhythmical energy unknown to past ages, and seem to many the foremost sculptors of our day. We wrote to both these and to James E. Fraser, designer of the bison and of some beauti-ful architectural sculpture, and to Publio Morbiducci, designer of the coin with the Fascist emblem, but Fraser refused, and Mestrovic did not reply until it was too late.* We substituted for Fraser the Ameri-can sculptor Manship, the creator of a Diana and her dogs, stylised and noble. But as yet we had no Englishman, and could think of no one among the well-known names that we admired both as sculptor and medallist. After some hesitation, for Charles Ricketts had recommended S. W. Carline, designer of a powerful Zeebrugge medal, and of a charm-

---

* We had written to a wrong address and our letter took some time reaching him. He made one magnificent design and, on discovering that the date had passed, gave it to the Irish Free State with great generosity.—W. B. Y.

ing medal struck to the honour of Flinders Petrie, we selected, on the recommendation of the Secretary of the British School at Rome, Percy Metcalfe, a young sculptor as yet but little known.

V

Because when an artist takes up a task for the first time he must sometimes experiment before he has mastered the new technique, we advised that the artist himself should make every alteration necessary, and that, if he had to go to London or elsewhere for the purpose, his expenses should be paid. An Irish artist had made an excellent design for the seal of the Dublin National Gallery, and that design, founded upon the seal of an Irish abbey, had been altered by the Mint, round academic contours substituted for the planes and straight lines of a mediaeval design. One remembers the rage of Blake when his designs came smooth and lifeless from the hands of an engraver whose work had been substituted for his. The Deputy Master of the Mint has commended and recommended to other nations a precaution which protects the artist, set to a new task and not as yet a craftsman, from the craftsman who can never be an artist.

VI

We refused to see the designs until we saw them all together. The name of each artist, if the model had been signed, was covered with stamp paper. The models were laid upon tables, with the exception of one set, fastened to a board, which stood upright on the mantelpiece. We had expected to recognise the work of the different artists by its style, but we recognised only the powerful handling of Milles on the board over the mantelpiece. One set of designs seemed far to exceed the others as decorations filling each its circular space, and this set, the work of Percy Metcalfe, had so marked a style, and was so excellent throughout, that it seemed undesirable to mix its designs with those of any other artist. Though we voted coin by coin, I think we were all convinced of this. I was distressed by my conviction. I had been certain that we could mix the work of three or four different artists, and that this would make our coinage more interesting, and had written to Milles, or to some friend of his, that it was unthinkable that we should not take at least one coin from so great an artist. Nobody could lay aside without a pang so much fine work, and our Government, had it invited designs, without competition, from either Morbiducci or Manship, would have been lucky to get such work as theirs. Manship's Ram and Morbiducci's Bull are magnificent; Manship's an entirely new creation, Morbiducci's a re-creation of the Bull on the Greek coin we had sent him as an example. That I may understand the energy and imagination of the designs of Milles I tell myself that they have been dug out of Sicilian earth, that they passed to and fro in the Mediterranean traffic two thousand years and more ago, and thereupon I discover that his strange bull, his two horses, that angry woodcock, have a supernatural energy. But all are cut in high relief, all suggest more primitive dies than we use to-day, and turned into coins would neither pitch nor pack.

What can I say of the Irish artists who had all done well in some department of their craft—Sheppard's "O'Leary" at the Municipal Gallery, and Power's "Kettle" at the Dublin National Gallery, are known, and Connor's "Emmet" may become known—except that had some powerful master of design been brought to Dublin years ago, and set to teach there, Dublin would have made a better show? Sir William Orpen affected Dublin painting, not merely because he gave it technical knowledge, but because he brought into a Dublin Art School the contagion of his vigour. The work of Metcalfe, Milles, Morbiducci, Manship, displays the vigour of their minds, and the forms of their designs symbolise that vigour, and our own is renewed at the spectacle.

As certain of the beasts represent our most important industry, they were submitted to the Minister for Agriculture and his experts, and we awaited the results with alarm. I have not been to Chartres Cathedral for years, but remember somewhere outside the great door figures of angels or saints, whose spiritual dignity and architectural effect depend upon bodies much longer in proportion to the length of their heads than a man's body ever was. The artist who must fill a given space and suggest some spiritual quality or rhythmical movement finds it necessary to suppress or exaggerate. Art, as some French critic has said, is appropriate exaggeration. The expert on horse-flesh, or bull-flesh, or swine-flesh, on the other hand, is bound to see his subject inanimate and isolated. The coins have suffered less than we feared. The horse, as first drawn, was more alive than the later version, for when the hind legs were brought more under the body and the head lowered, in obedience to technical opinion, it lost muscular tension; we passed from the open country to the show-ground. But, on the other hand, it is something to know that we have upon our half-crown a representation of an Irish hunter, perfect in all its points, and can add the horseman's pleasure to that of the children and the artists. The first bull had to go, though one of the finest of all the designs, because it might have upset, considered as an ideal, the eugenics of the farm-yard, but the new bull is as fine, in a different way. I sigh, however, over the pig, though I admit that the state of the market for pig's cheeks made the old design impossible. A design is like a musical composition, alter some detail and all has to be altered. With the round cheeks of the pig went the lifted head, the look of insolence and of wisdom, and the comfortable round bodies of the little pigs. We have instead querulous and harassed animals, better merchandise but less living.

VIII

I have given here my own opinions and impressions, and I have no doubt my Committee differs from some, but I know no other way of writing. We had all our points of view, though I can only remember one decision that was not unanimous. A member had to be out-voted because he wanted to substitute a harrier for a wolf-hound on the ground that on the only occasion known to him when hare and wolf-hound met the wolf-hound ran away. I am sorry that our meetings have come to an end, for we learned to like each other well.

What remains to be said is said in the name of the whole Committee. Our work could not have been done so quickly nor so well had not the Department of Finance chosen Mr. McCauley for our Secretary. Courteous, able and patient he has a sense of order that fills me with wonder.

W. B. YEATS

From Coinage of Saorstat Eireann, *Dublin, The Stationery Office,* *1928, 1-7.*

THE CHILD AND THE STATE

Speech made to the Irish Literary Society on November 30, 1925.

PERHAPS there are some here, one or two, who were present some thirty-six years ago at a meeting in my house, at which this society was first proposed. I think that meeting was the beginning of what is called the Irish Literary Movement. We and Dr. Hyde and his movement, which began three or four years later with the foundation of the Gaelic League, tried to be unpolitical, and yet all that we did was dominated by the political situation. Whether we wrote speeches, or wrote poems, or wrote romances or wrote books of history, we could not get out of our heads that we were somehow pleading for our country before a packed jury. And that meant a great deal of strain, a great deal of unreality, and even a little hysteria. Now there is no one to win over. Ireland has been put into our hands that we may shape it, and I find all about me in Ireland today a new overflowing life. To this overflowing life I attribute that our audiences at the Abbey Theatre have doubled, that the interest in music is so great that the Royal Dublin Society, which a few years ago was content with a hall that held seven hundred people, finds its new hall that holds some fifteen hundred so much too small, that every afternoon concert has to be repeated in the evening. Nor is it only appreciation that has grown, for where there is the right guidance and the right discipline, young men are ready for the hardest work. Colonel Brase does not find it hard to get his young men to practise many hours a day, his difficulty is sometimes to get them to cease work.

I know no case where the best teaching has been brought to Ireland in vain, and to-day there is a greater desire than ever before for expression, I think I may also say for discipline. The whole nation is plastic and receptive, but it is held back, and will be held back for some time to come by its lack of education, education in the most common and necessary subjects.

For that reason I put so much reliance in your patriotism and your patience that I am going to talk to you about education in the Primary Schools. Perhaps, indeed, I but speak of it because it is so running in my head that I would speak badly of anything else. I have been going round schools listening at a school attendance committee, talking to schoolmasters and inspectors. Many of you have influence in Ireland, influence through the Press, or through your friends, and I want to impress upon you that the schools in Ireland are not fit places for children. They are insanitary, they are out of repair, they are badly heated, and in Dublin and Cork they are far too small. The Government inherited this state of things, this old scandal; they want to put it right, but they will not be able to do so unless public opinion is with them, above all perhaps, unless just the kind of people who are here to-night are prepared to defend them and support them. The Government is introducing a Compulsory Education Bill, but we have all our individual responsibility, and we must see to it that compulsory education does not come into force—I do not say does not pass—until those schools are fitted for their work. And if the children are going to be forced to school you must not only see that those schools are warm and clean and sanitary, but you must do as other countries are doing more and more, and see that children during school hours are neither half-naked nor starved.

You cannot do this by money alone, you must create some body of men with knowledge, that can give enough attention to see that all does not go to ruin again. Many of us think that you can only accomplish this by having a county rate struck, and by having county committees to supervise the spending of the money. No one proposes to interfere with the present manager's right to appoint and dismiss teachers. That right is cherished by the clergy of all denominations, but the ablest managers would, I believe, welcome popular control if confined to heating, housing, clothing, cleaning, etc. The old system has broken down, and all know that it has.

Only when the schools have been made habitable will the question arise that most interests us—what are you going to teach there? Whether Gaelic be compulsory or voluntary, a great deal of it will be taught. At present Gaelic scholars assure me that there is nothing to read in modern Irish except for very young children who love fairy-tales. You must translate, you must modernise. A Committee of the Senate, of which I was chairman, has made a recommendation to the Government asking it to endow research into old, middle and modern Irish. Nothing is decided, but I think the Government will make this grant. Probably most of the books so produced will be in middle or ancient Irish, and in any case unsuitable for young children. They will, however, supply the material from which in some degree a vivid modern literature may be created. I think the Government should appoint some committee of publication and so make possible a modern Gaelic literature. Let us say, Dr. Douglas Hyde, Mr. James Stephens, who is always working at his Irish, and Mr. Robin Flower, who is a great scholar and a fine critic. They would not have time to do much of the great work themselves, but they could put others to it. Up to, say, ten years old, a child is content with a wild old tale, but from ten years on you must give it something with more of the problems of life in it. I would like to see the great classics, especially of the Catholic Latin nations, translated into Gaelic.

The tendency of the most modern education, that in Italy, let us say, is to begin geography with your native fields, arithmetic by counting the school chairs and measuring the walls, history with local monuments, religion with the local saints, and then to pass on from that to the nation itself. That is but carrying into education principles a group of artists, my father among them, advocated in art teaching. These artists have said: "Do not put scholars to draw from Greek or Roman casts until they have first drawn from life; only when they have drawn from life can they understand the cast." That which the child sees—the school—the district—and to a lesser degree the nation—is like the living body: distant countries and everything the child can only read of is like the cold Roman or Greek cast. If your education therefore is efficient in the modern sense, it will be more national than the dreams of politicians. If your education is to be effective you must see to it that your English teaching also begins with what is near and familiar. I suggest therefore another commission or committee to find writers who can create English reading books and history books, which speak of Ireland in simple vivid language. Very few such books exist, indeed I can only think of Mr. Standish O'Grady's *Bog of Stars,* published at the suggestion of this Society many years ago. That book is a fine piece of writing, and the books I think of should be fine pieces of writing, written by men of letters, chosen by men of letters; yet I do not think that I would exclude from the children's books any simple masterpiece of English literature. Let them begin with their own, and then pass to the world and the classics of the world.

There are two great classics of the eighteenth century which have deeply influenced modern thought, great Irish classics too difficult to be taught to children of any age, but some day those among us who think that all things should begin with the nation and with the genius of the nation, may press them upon the attention of the State. It is impossible to consider any modern philosophical or political question without being influenced knowingly or unknowingly by movements of thought that originated with Berkeley, who founded the Trinity College Philosophical Society, or with Burke, who founded the Historical. It would be but natural if they and those movements were studied in Irish colleges, perhaps especially in those colleges where our teachers themselves are trained. The Italian Minister of Education has advised his teachers continually to study the great classics, and he adds that those great classics will be as difficult to them as is the lesson to the child, and will therefore help them to understand the mind of a child.

In Gaelic literature we have something that the English-speaking countries have never possessed—a great folk literature. We have in Berkeley and in Burke a philosophy on which it is possible to base the whole life of a nation. That, too, is something which England, great as she is in modern scientific thought and every kind of literature, has not, I think. The modern Irish intellect was born more than two hundred years ago when Berkeley defined in three or four sentences the mechanical philosophy of Newton, Locke and Hobbes, the philosophy of England in his day, and I think of England up to our day, and wrote after each "We Irish do not hold with this," or some like sentence.

Feed the immature imagination upon that old folk life, and the mature intellect upon Berkeley and the great modern idealist philosophy created by his influence, upon Burke who restored to political thought its sense of history, and Ireland is reborn, potent, armed and wise. Berkeley proved that the world was a vision, and Burke that the State was a tree, no mechanism to be pulled in pieces and put up again, but an oak tree that had grown through centuries.

Teacher after teacher in Ireland has said to me that the young people are anarchic and violent, and that we have to show them what the State is and what they owe to it. All over the world during the Great War the young people became anarchic and violent, but in Ireland it is worse than elsewhere, for we have in a sense been at war for generations, and of late that war has taken the form of burning and destruction under the eyes of the children. They respect nothing, one teacher said to me. "I cannot take them through Stephen's Green because they would pull up the plants." Go anywhere in Ireland and you will hear the same complaint. The children, everybody will tell you, are individually intelligent and friendly, yet have so little sense of their duty to community and neighbour that if they meet an empty house in a lonely place they will smash all the windows. Some of the teachers want lessons on "Civic Duty," but there is much experience to show that such lessons, being of necessity dry and abstract, are turned to mockery. The proper remedy is to teach religion, civic duty and history as all but inseparable. Indeed, the whole curriculum of a school should be as it were one lesson and not a mass of unrelated topics. I recommend Irish teachers to study the attempt now being made in Italy, under the influence of their Minister of Education, the philosopher Gentile, the most profound disciple of our own Berkeley, to so correlate all subjects of study. I would have each religion, Catholic or Protestant, so taught that it permeate the whole school life, and that it may do so, that it may be good education as well as good religion, I would have it taught upon a plan signed, as it is in Italy, by the representative of the Government as well as by the religious authority. For instance, the Italian teachers are directed by the Minister to teach "no servile fear." Up to three years ago in Ireland religion could not be taught in school hours, and even now, though that regulation is no longer binding, it is often nothing but a daily lesson in the Catechism. In Italy it takes four forms, that it may not be abstract, and that it may be a part of history and of life itself, a part, as it were, of the foliage of Burke's tree. First, praying, the learning and saying of simple prayers; second, singing, the learning and singing of famous religious songs; third, narration, the reading, or perhaps among the younger children the hearing, and writing out in the child's own words of stories out of the Bible, and stories of the great religious personages of their own country; fourth, contemplation, by which I mean that dogmatic teaching which stirs the mind to religious thought. The prayers and songs for an Irish school exist in abundance. There are, for instance, many religious songs in Gaelic with their traditional music, and they are already published in little books.

Every child in growing from infancy to maturity should pass in imagination through the history of its own race and through something of the history of the world, and the most powerful part in that history is played by religion. Let the child go its own way when maturity comes, but it is our business that it has something of that whole inheritance, and not as a mere thought, an abstract thing like those Graeco-Roman casts upon the shelves in the art-schools, but as part of its emotional life.

One never knows where one's words carry, and I, in speaking, though I speak to you all, am thinking perhaps of some one young man or some one young girl who may hear my words and bear them in mind years hence. Even he and she may do nothing with my thought, but they may carry it, or some other amongst you may carry it, as a bird will carry a seed clinging to its claws. I am thinking of an Egyptian poem, where there are birds flying from Arabia with spice in their claws. I do not think any of you are millionaires, and yet permit me to dream that my words may reach one that is. If the Government were to do all that I suggest, if after the schools are put in good repair it were to get together the right editors and they find the right authors, if all the textbooks necessary to create a religious and secular culture in Irish and English were published, there would still be much that no Government, certainly no Government of a poor country, can accomplish. England has had great educational endowments for centuries, everyone knows with what lavish generosity the rich men of America have endowed education. Large sums of money have been sent to Ireland for political ends, and rich Irish-Americans have largely contributed, and we all hope, I think, that there is no further need for that money. If societies like this interest themselves in Irish education and spread that interest among the Irish educated classes everywhere, money may be sent to us to cheapen the price of school-books for the poor, or to clothe the poorer children, or to make the school buildings pleasanter to a child's eyes, or in some other way to prepare for an Ireland that will be healthy, vigorous, orderly, and above all, happy.

W. B. YEATS

From The Irish Statesman, *December, 1925, 393-94; 425.*

Appendix V

THE IRISH CENSORSHIP

Yeats retired from the Senate on September 28, 1928, just a few days before the Senate debate on the "Censorship of Publications Bill." On September 29, however, there appeared an article in The Spectator *by Yeats attacking the Bill; and it seems obvious that that article would have formed the substance of his speech on censorship had he still been a member of the Senate. It is included here for that reason.*

THE other night I woke with a sense of well-being, of recovered health and strength. It took me a moment to understand that it had come to me because our men and women of intellect, long separated by politics, have in the last month found a common enemy and drawn together. Two days before I had gone to see an old friend, from whom I had been separated for years, and was met with the words, "We are of the same mind at last." The Free State Government has in a month accomplished what would, I had thought, take years, and this it has done by drafting a Bill which it hates, which must be expounded and defended by Ministers full of contempt for their own words.

Ecclesiastics, who shy at the modern world as horses in my youth shied at motor-cars, have founded a "Society of Angelic Welfare." Young men stop trains armed with automatics and take from the guard's van bundles of English newspapers. Some of these ecclesiastics are of an incredible ignorance. A Christian Brother publicly burnt an

English magazine because it contained the Cherry Tree Carol, the lovely celebration of Mary's sanctity and her Child's divinity, a glory of the mediaeval church as popular in Gaelic as in English, because, scandalised by its naivete, he believed it the work of some irreligious modern poet; and this man is so confident in the support of an ignorance even greater than his own, that a year after his exposure in the Press, he permitted, or directed his society to base an appeal for public support, which filled the front page of a principal Dublin newspaper, upon the destruction of this "infamous" poem.

> "Then out and spoke that little Babe,
>   which was within Her womb;
> 'Bow down, bow down thou cherry tree
>   And give my Mother some.'"

The Bill is called "Censorship of Publications Bill, 1928," and empowers the Minister of Justice to appoint five persons, removable at his pleasure, who may, if that be his pleasure, remain for three years apiece, and to these persons he may on the complaint of certain "recognised associations" (The Catholic Truth Society and its like) submit for judgment book or periodical. These five persons must then say whether the book or periodical is "indecent," which word "shall be construed as including calculated to excite sexual passions or to suggest or incite to sexual immorality or in any other way to corrupt or deprave," or whether, if it be not "indecent" it inculcates "principles contrary to public morality," or "tends to be injurious or detrimental to or subversive of public morality." If they decide it is any of these things the Minister may forbid the post to carry it, individual or shop or library to sell or lend it. The police are empowered by another section to go before a magistrate who will be bound by the Bill's definition of the word "indecent" and obtain, without any reference to the committee or the Minister, a right to seize in a picture-dealer's shop, or at a public exhibition where the pictures are for sale, an Etty, or a Leighton—the police have already objected to "The Bath of

Psyche"—and fine or imprison the exhibitor. Another section forbids the sale or distribution of any "appliances to be used for," or any book or periodical which advocates or contains an advertisement of any book or periodical which advocates "birth control." The *Spectator*, the *Nation*, the *New Statesman*, and *Nature*, are, I understand, liable to seizure.

This Bill, if it becomes law, will give one man, the Minister of Justice, control over the substance of our thought, for its definition of "indecency" and such vague phrases as "subversive of public morality," permit him to exclude *The Origin of Species*, Karl Marx's *Capital*, the novels of Flaubert, Balzac, Proust, all of which have been objected to somewhere on moral grounds, half the Greek and Roman Classics, Anatole France and everybody else on the Roman index, and all great love poetry. The Government does not intend these things to happen, the Commission on whose report the Bill was founded did not intend these things to happen, the holy gunmen and "The Society of Angelic Welfare" do not intend all these things to happen; but in legislation intention is nothing, and the letter of the law everything, and no Government has the right, whether to flatter fanatics or in mere vagueness of mind to forge an instrument of tyranny and say that it will never be used. Above all, they have no right to say it here in Ireland, where until the other day the majority of children left school at twelve years old, and where even now, according to its own inspectors, no primary schoolmaster opens a book after school hours.

It will, of course, appoint a "reasonable committee," and, unless the Minister of Justice decides to remove one or more of its members, four out of five must agree before anything happens. I know those reasonable committee-men who have never served any cause but always make common cause against the solitary man of imagination or intellect. Had such a committee, with even those two Protestant clergymen upon it somebody suggests, censored the stage a while back, my theatre, now the State Theatre, would never have survived its first years. It now performs amid popular applause four plays, of which two, when first performed, caused riots, three had to be protected by the police, while all four had to face the denunciations of Press and pulpit. Speaking from the stage, I told the last rioters—to-day's newspaper burners— that they were not the first to rock the cradle of a man of genius. By such conflict truth, whether in science or in letters, disengages itself from the past. The present Bill does not affect us, but if it passes into law the next will bring the stage under a mob censorship acting through "recognized associations."

The well-to-do classes practise "birth control" in Ireland as else-where, and the knowledge is spreading downwards, but the Catholic Church forbids it. If those men of science are right, who say that in a hundred years the population will overtake the food supply, it will doubtless direct the married to live side by side and yet refrain from one another, a test it has not imposed upon monk and nun, and if they do not obey—well, Swift's "Modest Proposal" remains, and that, at any rate, would make love self-supporting.

Although it was almost certain that Catholic Ireland, thinking "birth control" wrong in principle, would follow the lead of countries that, being in sore need of soldiers and cheap labour, think it unde-sirable and legislate against it, those who belong to the Church of Ireland or to neither Church should compel the fullest discussion. The Government is forbidden under the Treaty to favour one religion at the expense of another, which does not mean that they may not pro-pose legislation asked for by one Church alone, but that they must show that the welfare of the State demands it. "You Mohammedans must not quote your Koran because the Christians do not believe in it, you Christians must not quote your Bible," said the chairman at the religious meeting in ancient Damascus—or was it Bagdad?—which scandalised the Spanish Traveller. Those who think it wrong to bring into the world children they cannot clothe and educate, and yet refuse to renounce that "on which the soul expands her wing," can say "no man knows whether the child is for love's sake, the fruit for the flower, or love for the child's sake, the flower for the fruit"; or quote the words of St. Thomas: "Anima est in toto corpore."

The enthusiasts who hold up trains are all the better pleased because the newspapers they burn are English, and their best public support has come from a newspaper that wants to exclude its rivals; but their motives may be, in the main, what they say they are, and great numbers of small shopkeepers and station-masters who vaguely disapprove of their methods approve those motives. A Government official said of these station-masters and shopkeepers the other day: "They are defending their sons and daughters and cannot understand why the good of the nine-tenths, that never open a book, should not prevail over the good of the tenth that does." Twenty years ago illegitimacy was almost unknown, infanticide unknown, and now both are common and increasing, and they think that if they could exclude English newspapers, with their police-court cases which excite the imagination, their occasional allusions to H. G. Wells which excite the intellect, their advertisements of books upon birth control which imply safety for illicit love, innocence would return. They do not understand that you cannot unscramble eggs, that every country passing out of automatism passes through demoralization, and that it has no choice but to go on into intelligence. I know from plays rejected by the Abbey Theatre that the idealist political movement has, after achieving its purpose, collapsed and left the popular mind to its own lawless vulgarity. Fortunately, the old movement created four or five permanent talents.

There are irresponsible moments when I hope that the Bill will pass in its present form, or be amended by the Republicans, as some foretell, into a still more drastic form, and force all men of intellect, who mean to spend their lives here, into a common understanding. One modern-minded Catholic writer has been hawking a letter round the Press threatening anti-clericalism; but if that come, and I do not expect it in my time, it will not come in the old form. No Irishman wants the fourteenth century, even though most damnably compromised and complicated by modern Rathmines, driven from his back door so long as the front door opens on the twentieth. Our imaginative movement has its energy from just that combination of new and old, of old stories, old poetry, old belief in God and the soul, and a modern technique. A certain implacable and able Irish revolutionary soldier put me to read Berkeley with the phrase: "There is all the philosophy a man needs"; and I have long held that intellectual Ireland was born when Berkeley wrote in that famous note-book of his after an analysis of contemporary mechanistic thought: "We Irish do not think so," or some such words. The power to create great character or possess it cannot long survive the certainty that the world is less solid than it looks and the soul much solider—"a spiritual substance" in some sense or other—and our dramatists, when they leave Ireland, or get away from the back door in some other fashion, prefer cause or general idea to characters that are an end to themselves and to each other. Synge's "Playboy" and O'Casey's "Plough and the Stars" were attacked because, like "The Cherry Tree Carol," they contain what a belief, tamed down into a formula, shudders at, something wild and ancient.

From The Spectator, *September, 29, 1928, 391-92.*

INDEX